Hospitality : Recipes
And Entertainment
Hints For All Occasions

Wright, Mary M. (Mary Mason), b. 1870

HOSPITALITY

BY

MARY M. WRIGHT

AUTHOR OF

"CANDY MAKING AT HOME"
"PRESERVING AND PICKLING"
"SALADS AND SANDWICHES"
"DAINTY DESSERTS"

RECIPES AND ENTER-
TAINMENT HINTS FOR
ALL OCCASIONS

PHILADELPHIA
THE PENN PUBLISHING COMPANY
1922

Contents

CONTENTS

CONTENTS

Hospitality

I

HOSPITALITY FOR HOLIDAYS

CHAPTER I

HOSPITALITY FOR HOLIDAYS

TABLE DECORATIONS FOR NEW YEAR'S DAY

VERY effective decorations for the New Year's tables may be charmingly carried out with red, silver and gold bells. If a red scheme is carried out use as a centerpiece a red floral bell, or a bell of holly with a clapper of mistletoe. This bell should be suspended from the light fixtures over the table, or in case you do not have overhead lights they may be suspended from a tripod made of three sticks covered with green crepe paper and evergreen. Red bell-shaped bonbons may be at each plate. The place-cards may be decorated with red bells either cut out of crepe paper or post-cards, and appliqued onto plain cards, or those with the edges touched up with a little red. A novel effect may be obtained by suspending red crepe bells over the table by

15

means of fine black thread. They may be suspended directly from the ceiling, or from cords stretched from one wall to the other, several inches below the ceiling.

A pretty way in which to decorate a New Year's table with either gold or silver bells is to suspend a shower of them over the table, using narrow ribbon, or silver or gold tinsel to suspend by. If silver bells are used have for a centerpiece a silver bowl, or silvered basket filled with pink, white, or blue blossoms. If gilt bells are used then have a pale blue basket filled with yellow blossoms and delicate ferns, or a yellow basket with white blossoms. If candles are used it would be nice to have the shades trimmed with a fringe of tiny bells. For place-cards decorate plain gilt-edged cards with gilt bells, which may be painted or appliqued on, or a tiny bell could be tied in one corner of the card, using gilt or tinsel cord or very narrow white ribbon to tie it on with. If a silver bell scheme is used silver-edged cards decorated with silver bells should be used.

Another effective bell scheme is to cover a

hoop with silver or gilt paper, according to the kind of bells to be used. Fasten tiny bells all around the hoop by means of silver or gilt cord. If you wish something more elaborate have streamers of white or yellow ribbons, studded with tiny silver or gilt bells, to reach from the hoop to the plates where they may be attached to bell-shaped bonbon boxes.

Another unique centerpiece for a bell luncheon is a little belfry formed of small blossoms and vines arranged over a pasteboard foundation. Suspend from the belfry a tiny gilt or silver bell, and have a silver or gilt cord attached to the hand of the doll dressed to represent Father Time.

New Year Bell Luncheons
(*With Red Bells*)
Pimiento Canapes (Bell-shaped)
Bell-shaped Salmon Croquettes   Bell-shaped Sandwiches
Potato Salad (Garnished with Beet Bells)
Cherry Gelatin (Molded in bell-shape)
Loaf Cake (Decorated with red bells made of
Candied Cherries)
Bonbons in Red Paper Bells

(With Silver Bells)

Clear Bouillon
Creamed Chicken in Timbale Bells
Bell-shaped Potato Croquettes   Bell-shaped Sandwiches
Fruit Salad (Garnished with Candied Pineapple Bells)
Ice-Cream Bells   Macaroon Bells·
Angel Food Cake (Decorated with Silver Candy Bells

(With Gold Bells)

Orange Fruit Cup
Fish in Lemon Bells   Carrot Bells (Creamed)
Bell Corn Muffins   Golden Sirup
Fruit Salad (Garnished with Banana Bells)
Ice-Cream Bells   Cup Cakes
Bell Bonbons

PIMIENTO CANAPES

Pimientoes	Bread
Cream cheese	Tomato catsup

Slice the bread thin, and cut into shape of bells and toast a delicate brown in the oven. Butter the bread and cover with a mixture of cream cheese and catsup, seasoned with salt and paprika. Place on top bells cut out of the pimientoes—just made to fit the toasted bells.

BELL-SHAPED SALMON CROQUETTES

1 can red salmon
Salt and paprika
Egg

1 cupful thick tomato sauce
Bread-crumbs

Empty the salmon from the can and remove all skin and bones, and flake. Add the tomato sauce made by blending together in a double boiler two tablespoonfuls each of butter and flour, then stirring in one cupful of tomato purée. Season with salt and paprika. Set aside to cool, then form into shape of bells, roll in egg, and then in bread-crumbs, and fry in deep fat. Serve hot in a bed of parsley.

POTATO SALAD GARNISHED WITH BEET BELLS

Cold boiled beets
1 onion
Mayonnaise or boiled
  dressing

Hard-boiled eggs
Celery
Pickled beets

Peel and cut the potatoes up in cubes. To a quart of the potatoes, add one onion chopped fine, one cupful chopped celery and three hard-boiled eggs chopped fine. Mix thoroughly, seasoning with salt, pepper and salad dressing. Line a salad dish with lettuce leaves and place the salad in this, heaping up in mound shape. Cut little bells out of pickled beets and garnish the salad with these.

CHERRY GELATIN IN BELL-SHAPE

1 tablespoonful gelatin	1 pint cherry juice
1 cupful canned cherries	½ cupful cold water
½ cupful sugar	Candied cherries

Place the sugar in the cherry juice (use red cherries) and bring to the boil; then stir in the gelatin that has been dissolved in the cold water. Add the cherries after they have been stoned. Pour into bell molds, or if you cannot obtain these use wine glasses or glasses that slope toward a point, or egg-shells with opening made at one end, may be used. Set on ice to chill and when ready to serve turn out. Use candied cherries for handles and also for the clappers of the bells.

A DATE LUNCHEON

Date and Grapefruit Cup

Date Sandwiches   Olives

Sautéd Dates with Cream Cheese

Chicken Croquettes   Date Salad

Ice-Cream   Maple Date Cake

Have this menu printed on the backs of tiny calendars, and place one at each plate. If you have a small palm tree tie on it bunches of stuffed dates, and use for a centerpiece.

At each plate have fancy baskets or boxes filled with stuffed dates. Baskets in dull red would add a bit of color to the table that would be effective. Have the date of the year on the place-cards, and if liked they may be decorated with tiny calendars.

DATE AND GRAPEFRUIT CUP

1 pound best dates   3 grapefruits

2 oranges   Sirup

Stone and cut the dates into bits. Cut the grapefruits in halves and remove the pulp. Break up into bits and shred the orange pulp. Mix with the dates. Make a sirup with pine-apple and orange juice, and boil to the thickness of honey. Pour over the fruit. Chill on ice. Serve in grapefruit cups made out of halved rinds.

SAUTÉD DATES WITH CREAM CHEESE

Sauté the dates, after the stones have been removed, in hot butter, then when cool stuff with cream cheese—these are something new and greatly relished.

DATE SALAD

2 cupfuls chopped tart apples
1 cupful nut-meats

1 cupful stoned dates
Sirup dressing

Cut the dates up into bits, and mix with the apple and the chopped nut-meats. Blend thoroughly together; then dress with either a sirup dressing made with fruit juice and sugar, or with a mayonnaise dressing.

DATE SANDWICHES

1 cupful chopped dates
½ cupful chopped nut-meats

½ cupful chopped figs
Thick cream

Mix the dates, nut-meats and figs together,

and moisten with enough thick cream to make
of the right consistency to spread. Flavor
with a teaspoonful of vanilla. This filling is
good between thin slices of brown bread.

———

THE NEW YEAR DINNER

Menu No. 1

Oyster Soup

Roast Turkey with Celery Stuffing   Frozen Cranberries

Browned Potatoes   Corn Soufflé

Peas in Carrot or Turnip Cups

Fruit Salad

Confection Pie   Cream Cheese Balls

Cranberry Sponge with Marshmallow Border

Stuffed Fruits   Nuts   Bonbons

Coffee

Menu No. 2

Cream of Tomato Soup   Canapes

Roast Chicken with Dressing or Cooked en Casserole

Creamed Cauliflower

Browned Sweet Potatoes   Beet Pickles

Cranberry Salad in Cranberry Rings

Steamed Fruit Pudding or Frozen Plum Pudding

Ginger Sherbet

Crystallized Popcorn   Bonbons

Fruit Salad

2 large tart apples	¼ cup chopped nut-meats
1 pimiento	Custard with whipped cream
1 cup finely chopped celery	1 cup white grapes
Candied cherries or cranberries	½ cup red cherries

Peel and cut up the apple into cubes, add the grapes, halved and seeded, the canned cherries drained of all juice, the chopped nut-meats and the celery. Mix lightly together. Sprinkle very lightly with salt, sugar and a few drops of lemon-juice, then dress with a boiled-custard dressing in which a half-cup of whipped cream has been stirred. Garnish with candied cherries.

Confection Pie

3 lemons	4 eggs
1 quart milk	1 cup sugar
1 cup stale sponge or other yellow cake-crumbs	1 tablespoon corn-starch
	Candied sweetmeats

Pare the outer rind of the lemons and boil in a little water until tender, then pound to a paste and mix with the cake-crumbs; stir in the boiling milk. Beat the yolks of the eggs light, with the sugar, then add to them the juice of the lemons and blend the corn-starch in them also. Place the milk in a double boiler and stir in the egg-mixture, and stir until thick and smooth; then stir in the stiffly whipped egg-whites. Pour into two baked pie-shells, and strew the top thickly with candied sweet-meats, such as thinly sliced citron, orange rind, candied pineapple and cherries.

CRANBERRY SPONGE WITH MARSHMALLOW BORDER

2 eggs
1 cup sugar
3 teaspoons baking-powder
Cranberry jelly

1 cup milk
2 cups flour
1 teaspoon vanilla
Marshmallows

Make a sponge with the beaten eggs, milk, flour and sugar and baking-powder. Bake in one large round pan. Remove from the oven when done and ice with a white icing; while the cake and icing are still hot place the marshmallows around the edge of the sponge-cake. Fill the center of cake with a thick cranberry jelly. Press a candied cranberry or cherry into the center of each marshmallow if you wish to have the cake look more Christmassy. Serve with whipped cream.

STEAMED FIG PUDDING

½ cup shredded suet	Flour
1 cup bread-crumbs	1 cup shredded figs
1 cup light-brown sugar	2 cups milk
1 cup chopped nut-meats	1 orange
2 eggs	1 teaspoon baking-powder

Flour the figs and the nut-meats, then add to the suet. Soak the bread-crumbs in the milk, then add to them the beaten egg-yolks and the grated rind and the juice of the orange. Sift the baking-powder with one-half cup flour and stir in. If the dough is too soft add a little more flour. Stir the ingredients well together, lastly add the stiffly beaten egg-whites. Fill into buttered molds about two-thirds full and steam for two or three hours. Serve with a fruit or hard sauce.

FROZEN PLUM PUDDING

2 quarts chocolate ice-cream
½ glass orange marmalade
1 tablespoon candied cherries
¼ cup cooked raisins
½ glass strawberry preserves
2 tablespoons shaved citron
Ginger sherbet
¼ cup shredded figs

Stir the preserved and candied fruits into the chocolate ice-cream, then pack in ice and salt for two or three hours, so that the fruit flavors may be thoroughly blended with the cream.

To make the ginger sherbet, use a foundation as for lemon sherbet, then when partly frozen, stir in a large tablespoonful of Jamaica ginger and three tablespoons of sirup from preserved ginger. Stir in one cup of finely chopped nuts and the whipped whites of two eggs. Complete freezing. Place a layer of the frozen plum pudding in the bottom of sherbet glasses or other individual service dishes and top off with the ginger sherbet. Any dainty little cakes may be served with this dessert.

Table Decorations for Washington's Birthday

The decorations for Washington's birthday are nice carried out in the colonial blue and buff. If at all possible use the old-fashioned dark blue china on the table; but if you do not have this gold-banded china will do, or the imitation willowware. The question of table covering is easily and cheaply settled by purchasing the blue and white Japanese toweling with its characteristic designs. Have one runner of this toweling extending lengthwise of the table, and two or three strips running crossways; or if the table is square or round just have two strips crossing in the center of the table. Yellow roses or tulips would make an effective centerpiece if arranged in a deep blue bowl or basket. Yellow fruits may also be appropriately used as a centerpiece. Use a pretty blue basket, and heap up with yellow bananas and grapefruit.

Decorate the place-cards with golden eagles. Blue boxes or fancy little baskets filled with yellow bonbons will add to the effect. If candles are used have the old-fashioned gold or brass candlesticks, with dark blue shades; if liked the shades may be decorated with golden eagles.

MENUS FOR WASHINGTON'S BIRTHDAY LUNCHEONS

Menu No. 1

Cream of Carrot Soup in Blue Cups

Chicken Salad   Cherry-Almond Sandwiches

Cream Cheese Cannon Balls

Individual Custards in Blue Cups   Sponge Cake

Yellow Bonbons

Menu No. 2

Grapefruit Cup

Sweet Potato Croquettes   Celery Sandwiches

Egg Salad

Creamed Corn in Pastry Shells   Lady Washington Cake

Orange Macaroons   Salted Almonds

Menu No. 3—Cherry Menu

Tomato Bouillon

Hatchet-shaped Sandwiches   Salmon Loaf

Cherry-celery Salad

Cherry Sherbet   Cherry Cakes

Cherry Bonbons

Menu No. 4—Red, White, and Blue Menu

Cream of Corn Soup in Blue Cups

Deviled Lobster   Escalloped Potatoes

Beet Salad

Fairy Cones   Pimolas

Patriotic Cake   Ice-cream

White and Yellow Bonbons in Blue Boxes

CREAM OF CARROT SOUP

½ dozen carrots	1 quart boiling water
1 small onion	3 stalks celery
2 cupfuls milk	1 teaspoonful salt
1 tablespoonful butter	1 tablespoonful flour
Pinch of cayenne	

Scrape and slice the carrots, peel and slice the onion and cut the celery up into bits. Pour the boiling water over them, and let simmer slowly until tender. Rub the vegetables through a sieve, and then add to the liquid. Blend together in a double boiler the butter and flour, heat the milk and stir in, cook until smooth, then add the vegetable purée. Season with the salt and pepper. If too thick add a little more milk.

DEVILED LOBSTER

1 can lobster	2 tablespoonfuls butter
1 tablespoonful chutney	1 tablespoonful mustard
Bread-crumbs	Lemon and parsley

Melt the butter in a pan and add the lobster, the chutney and the made mustard and a few soft bread-crumbs. The lobster should be chopped fine. Stir until hot and well mixed, then place on bread rounds that have been fried in hot fat a delicate brown. Garnish each round with a slice of lemon and parsley. This mixture can be made in a chafing dish if preferred.

TOMATO BOUILLON

1 quart of tomatoes	1 quart milk
2 slices of onion	3 stalks of celery
½ bay leaf	2 cloves
2 peppercorns	1 teaspoonful soda
2 tablespoonfuls butter	1 tablespoonful flour

Make a white sauce with the butter, flour

and the milk. Stew the tomatoes with the onion, celery and spices for about twenty minutes. Rub through a sieve, and just before combining the tomato juice with the white sauce add the soda. Season with salt and pepper to taste, and a teaspoonful of sugar will improve it for most people. Serve toasted croutons with this, or crackers.

CHERRY SHERBET

1 quart cherry juice	2 cupfuls of sugar
2 egg-whites	1 tablespoonful gelatin
2 lemons	2 oranges

Add the sugar to the cherry juice, and heat to the boiling point, then stir in the gelatin that has been soaked in a little cold water; add the juice of the lemon and oranges and a teaspoonful of almond extract. Dilute the mixture with water until as sweet as desired and the strength liked, then strain and freeze. When nearly frozen, fold in the stiffly beaten egg-whites and a few of the cherries chopped very fine. Cover carefully and pack in ice and let stand for an hour or so before serving.

TABLE DECORATIONS FOR FOURTH OF JULY TABLES

It is nice to have the table decorations for the Fourth of July carried out in the patriotic colors, red, white and blue. It is advisable to use the red and white in the food, and the blue touch may be obtained by the use of blue china, or by garnishing the dishes with blue flowers.

A red, white and blue color scheme may be carried out very nicely with flowers. Red, white and blue bachelor buttons make very effective decorations. Use a bowl of these for a centerpiece, then have at each plate a little old-fashioned bouquet of these flowers. If liked these may be placed on flag mat. Another pretty floral decoration may be carried out in blue and white flowers with only a touch of red. Have in the center of the table a blue bowl filled with white blossoms. Place this on a red, white and blue mat. Have at each place a small white basket filled with the dainty blue forget-me-nots, pansies, larkspurs, or any blue flowers that are easily obtained. Tie to the handle of each of these little baskets a tiny bow of red ribbon, or a red firecracker. The white place-cards may have a touch of red around the edge and the guests' names may be written on in red ink. Decorate the cards with blue pansies, forget-me-nots or whatever blossoms are used on the table.

CHILDREN'S TABLES FOR THE FOURTH OF JULY

Flag decorations are always appropriate for a children's table on the Fourth of July. Silk flags may be set up in tripod fashion in the center of the table and at each end. Suspend from the chandelier over the table a ball of flags; this is made by sticking small flags closely together in a large apple or potato. The edge of the white table-cloth may be trimmed with tiny flags crossed two by two. Tiny flags may be appliqued onto white china with flour paste, and will be sure to please the children; they can also be appliqued onto white candle shades and will seem to wave in the light behind them. The place-cards can be decorated with a border of tiny flags. Nearly every dish can have a flag served with it in some way, and to crown the affair there may be a real flag cake, and the ice-cream may be molded and decorated to represent a flag.

MENUS AND RECIPES FOR THE FOURTH OF JULY

Red, White and Blue Menus

Iced Cherries   Pimiento Sandwiches
Salmon Croquettes with Potato Border
Stuffed Baked Tomatoes   Red and White Radishes
Celery Salad in Red Pepper Cases
Red Raspberry Sherbet   Angel Food Cake

Tomato Appetizer
Scalloped Potatoes in Blue Ramekins with Cheese Balls
Molded Chicken   Currant Jelly Sandwiches
Cherry Salad
Red Watermelon and White Ice-cream   Small Cakes
Red and White Bonbons

Cream of Tomato Soup
Chicken in Red Sweet Bell Peppers Baked
Tomato Sandwiches   Egg and Beet Salad
Chilled Rice with Fruit
Cake   Fourth of July Punch

ICED CHERRIES

Red cherries	Sugar
Almonds	Orange-juice

Drain the canned cherries of all juice. Pound the almonds to a paste and roll up into tiny balls and fill the holes in the cherries with these. Fill sherbet glasses half full of the stuffed cherries, then fill two-thirds full of orange and cherry juice mixed, well sweetened with sugar. Just before serving place a teaspoonful of finely chopped ice on top of each glass. The almonds should be blanched before being pounded to a paste, and flavored with a little cinnamon or almond extract.

BAKED STUFFED TOMATOES

Firm ripe tomatoes	2 cupfuls boiled chicken
1 cupful boiled rice	2 tablespoonfuls celery
1 tablespoonful onion-juice	1 teaspoonful chopped
Salt, pepper and butter	parsley

Use one tomato for each person, scoop out the seeds and part of the pulp. Sprinkle the inside of the tomatoes with salt and pepper.

Fill with the other ingredients, well-mixed. Chop the cold-boiled chicken into bits, also chop the celery and parsley (if liked the onion can be omitted), melt the butter before adding. Place the top slice on the tomatoes, place in a bake-pan with a little butter and bake until the tomatoes are tender.

RASPBERRY SHERBET

1 quart raspberries	3 lemons
1 pint water	2 cupfuls sugar
2 eggs	1 teaspoonful lemon extract

Cook the raspberries in the water and strain through a sieve, pressing as much of the pulp through as possible, add the sugar and the lemon-juice. Let cool, then pour into a freezer and freeze to a mushy consistency, then add the stiffly beaten whites of the eggs. If a tablespoonful of gelatin is added to the hot sirup it will give more body to the sherbet. Let stand several hours. Form or mold the sherbet, using a sherbet cup. Turn out onto a white plate and garnish with blue blossoms.

TOMATO APPETIZER

Small ripe tomatoes
Mayonnaise dressing
  (white)
Chopped parsley
Salt and pepper

Sweet red peppers
2 eggs (hard-boiled)
1 small onion
Parsley

Cut off the tops of the tomatoes, but do not peel. Scoop out some of the inside, and mix with part of this a little chopped red pepper, chopped parsley, one small onion and the eggs chopped very fine. Season with salt and pepper, and, if liked, with a little anchovy paste and the mayonnaise. Fill this mixture into the cavities of the tomatoes. Serve one to each guest on a white plate, and garnish with blue pansies, bachelor buttons or larkspur.

CHERRY SALAD

Red and white cherries
Sirup dressing

Almonds
Whipped cream

Seed the cherries and combine after filling the cavities with bits of almond nut-meats. Dress with a thick sirup dressing made of fruit juice and sugar boiled together (lemon,

cherry, orange or pineapple juice are all excellent for this purpose). Heap up on individual blue plates and surround with a border
of whipped cream.

RED WATERMELON WITH WHITE ICE-CREAM

Choose a nice long watermelon and slice
crosswise about an inch thick. Remove all the
green rind and the seeds, leaving a ring of red
melon. Place these slices on individual blue
plates and fill the inside with white ice-cream,
smoothing it level with the melon.

CHICKEN IN SWEET BELL PEPPERS (*baked*)

Cold cooked chicken	Bread-crumbs
Celery or parsley	Cream sauce
Salt and pepper	Sweet bell peppers

Cut a slice of the stem ends of the peppers
and remove the seeds. Chop up the chicken,
and to each cupful add one-half cupful of
cream sauce and one-half cupful bread-crumbs,
add the seasoning, chopping the celery or
parsley fine. Fill this mixture into the bell

peppers, place in a bake-pan with a little water or stock around them and bake until tender. Place one on individual plates of blue.

TABLE DECORATIONS FOR THANKS-GIVING

When arranging the decorations for the Thanksgiving table, try to make them as dainty and cheerful as possible. Every guest should aim to present to her guests a harmonious picture, one that will be remembered in years to come, even if the menu to be served is a simple one. There is such a wealth of material to choose from for decorations at this season of the year that one need not lack in this respect. All the fruits of Mother Earth can be appropriately used at this time and until you have tried you could never dream how charming are the effects produced by the grouping of yellow and rosy red apples; white, red and purple grapes; yellow and russet pears; oranges and bananas; or of melons;

glowing pumpkins; dark red cabbages; deep purple eggplant; bright red and green peppers; white stalked celery with its light green foliage; sprigs of parsley and cress. Then the different varieties of nuts and grains can be used effectively. The berries of the mountain-ash and bittersweet and brilliant sumach will lend a bit of charming color to the table, and the abundant foliage of the gayly tinted autumn leaves and the trailing vines will help to soften and mellow the whole.

If fruit is used for the centerpiece, it may be arranged in a number of effective ways. A large bowl, or basket with handle, may be fashioned out of a large pumpkin and filled with fruit. This should be placed on a mat of brilliant autumn leaves or grape leaves, interspersed with bittersweet berries. The edge of the basket and the handle, if a basket is used, should be wreathed with vines and red berries, or with chrysanthemums. If a pumpkin basket is used for the centerpiece, it would be charming to have at each corner of the table a shallow pumpkin basket containing nuts and candies; these baskets can be neatly lined with crepe paper. When a fruit centerpiece is used, the salad will be attractive served in rosy red apples hollowed out, while at each plate could be a bunch of glacé grapes.

A nice idea is to make a mat of brown and yellow maple leaves in the center of the table, and on this place a tub or basket fashioned out of a large pumpkin. Fill this with fruits. Place all around the base of the pumpkin yellow carrots with their green tops left on, or small beets may be used. Have all the vegetables used clean and shining. Fashion out of squashes horns of plenty, and have one at each end of the table, filled to overflowing with nuts. Vegetables or small pumpkins hollowed out and lined with paraffine paper will make good bonbon holders, or cases for the salads and ices.

THANKSGIVING TABLES FOR THE CHILDREN

When there is to be a family reunion or family party on Thanksgiving Day, and there are

to be a good many children among the guests,
it is advisable to plan for a separate table for
them. This not only saves much confusion,
but what is of still more importance, keeps
the children from eating rich foods that will
not be good for them that is being served to the
grown-ups. The children's tables should be as
carefully planned and decorated as the tables
for their elders.

A pretty table decoration for a children's
Thanksgiving table is made by covering a table
with a plain white oil-cloth, just cut to fit the
top of the table. All around the sides of the
table fasten a frill of crepe paper with a border
of turkeys. This kind of cover will suit a circular table best. Turkeys cut out of crepe
paper may be pasted in a circle around the
cloth just inside the plate line. If liked crepe
paper decorated with turkey may be used on
top of the table instead of the oil-cloth. A
large papier-mâché turkey with a cavity for
bonbons or nuts may be used for a centerpiece; or a little yard may be built with birch
bark, or twigs or pasteboard painted to repre-

sent boards.   Inside of the yard place a number of little papier-mâché turkeys; these may be obtained for from a few cents up to ten cents according to size.

THANKSGIVING DINNER MENUS

Menu No. 1

Cream of Tomato Soup
Turkey with Oyster Stuffing
Celery   Browned Sweet Potatoes
Stuffed Onions
Salad in Green and Red Pepper Cases
Pumpkin Pie   Strawberry Tarts   Mince Pie
Cranberry Sherbet   Raisin Nut Cakes
Fruit   Candies   Nuts
Coffee

Menu No. 2

Cream of Celery Soup
Turkey with Chestnut Stuffing
Riced Potatoes
Creamed Peas in Carrot Cups   Bean Salad in Beet Cups
Whipped Cranberry Jelly   Spiced Fruit
Pumpkin Pie   Apple Pie
Ginger Sponge
Nuts   Fruits
Coffee

Menu No. 3

Oyster Soup

Crackers   Pickles

Turkey with Sausage Stuffing

Cranberry Appetizer Ice

Baked Hubbard Squash   Scalloped Potatoes

Tomato Mushroom Salad

Caramel Pumpkin Pie   Apple Pie

Plum Pudding with Hard Sauce

Nuts   Fruits   Candies

Coffee

MENUS FOR THANKSGIVING DAY LUNCHEONS

Fruit Appetizer

Turkey Sandwiches   Tomato Nut Salad

Baked Stuffed Apples

Sweet Potato Croquettes

Pear Compote   Cocoanut Nut Cake

Popcorn Balls   Nut Candies

Coffee

Cream of Tomato and Celery Soup

Apple Date Salad   Tutti Frutti Sandwiches

Turkey Patties

Celery

Pumpkin Custards   Ginger Nut Cakes

Crystallized Popcorn

Fruits   Nuts

Coffee

Pressed Turkey   Sweet Corn Soufflés
                    Celery Rolls
        Cauliflower Pickle   Sweet Peach Pickles
                  Pumpkin Fanchonettes
Pineapple Sponge   Chocolate Nut Cake
                    Salted Almonds

Oyster Stuffing for Turkey

1 quart bread-crumbs	1 pint oysters
2 teaspoonfuls salt	½ teaspoonful pepper
1 tablespoonful chopped parsley	1 tablespoonful butter

Mix all well together, and stuff the turkey with this. If the turkey is large the ingredients can be increased to suit. Drain the juice from the oysters before measuring.

Stuffed Onions

Large white onions	Butter
Grated ham	Bread-crumbs
A little chopped parsley or celery	Salt and pepper

Remove the skins from the onions and parboil in slightly salted water for ten minutes. Drain and set aside to cool. Mix together some bread-crumbs, a little grated or finely chopped ham, a little of the onion removed from the center of the onions. Season and moisten with a little melted butter or cream. Fill this mixture into the cavities of the onions, after the centers of the onions have been removed. Sprinkle the top with buttered bread-crumbs, and bake in the oven until tender. Use about one-half cupful of ham to a cupful and a half of bread-crumbs.

BROWNED SWEET POTATOES

Boil sweet potatoes until tender, peel, and lay in roasting-pan close to the turkey for the last half hour, or until browned.

CRANBERRY SHERBET

1 quart cranberry-juice   Juice of five oranges
2 pounds granulated sugar   1 pint water
4 egg-whites

Place the water and sugar over the fire and cook until all the sugar is dissolved; then add the cranberry juice and the juice of the oranges. If too strong add a little more water. Pour into an ice-cream freezer and freeze to a mushy consistency. Whip the whites of the eggs very stiff and stir into the cranberry mixture, then complete the freezing without stirring.

CREAM OF CELERY SOUP

1 dozen stalks of celery	3 cupfuls of water
½ onion	A bay leaf
A bit of mace	2 or 3 peppercorns
2 cupfuls milk	Salt and pepper
1 tablespoonful butter	1 tablespoonful flour
1 cupful cream	½ teaspoonful sugar

Wash the celery stalks thoroughly and break into small pieces, put over the fire with the water, onion and other spices, and let simmer very slowly for an hour. Then pass through a coarse sieve. Make a thin sauce with the flour, butter and milk heated. When smooth, season, add the celery purée, and lastly stir in the cream. Blend all well together and serve in boullion cups with croutons or wafers.

CARAMEL-PUMPKIN PIE

1 pint steamed pumpkin	1 pint good milk
3 eggs	2 tablespoonfuls butter
1 cupful brown sugar	1 teaspoonful vanilla

Place in a stew-pan the butter and the sugar and heat to the caramel stage, but be careful not to scorch. Remove from the fire and add one pint of steamed pumpkin which has been passed through a colander, add the milk, the egg, well-beaten, and the flavoring. Line deep pie tins with good pie pastry, pour in the pumpkin mixture and bake a nice brown.

PLUM PUDDING

1 cupful flour	1 teaspoonful baking-powder
1 cupful brown sugar	1½ cupfuls bread-crumbs
1 cupful raisins	1 cupful chopped suet
½ cupful chopped citron	1 cupful currants
½ teaspoonful allspice, nutmeg, and salt	¼ cupful chopped almonds
	4 eggs
Grated rind of one lemon	½ cupful grape-juice
1 cupful milk	½ teaspoonful soda

Mix the dry ingredients thoroughly together, and the liquid ingredients also thoroughly together, adding the soda last dissolved in a little water. Stir the liquid into the dry ingredients. Turn this into a mold and steam six hours. This makes a very large pudding. Serve with a hard sauce or a fruit sauce.

TABLE DECORATIONS FOR CHRISTMAS

Every home should be decorated for the merry holiday season. Especially should this be true of the dining-room and the table around which the festivities circle. These decorations need not be elaborate, but can be simple and artistic. Red and green are called the Christmas colors; the other colors that are especially suitable for Christmas are white, the emblem of purity, and yellow, which signifies joy and happiness.

A red and green basket scheme makes a very effective table decoration for the Christmas season, and need not be expensive. A basket can be painted a deep red and filled with trailing vines and ferns; this basket, if not too large, may be suspended over the center of the table, with the vines trailing down on the cloth. Have at each plate little evergreen baskets filled with red blossoms, or they can be lined with waxed paper and filled with red bonbons. An evergreen basket filled with red blossoms makes a pretty centerpiece. From the basket fine ropes of evergreen may extend to the four corners of the table, and there tied to other smaller baskets. An evergreen basket filled with ruddy red apples may be substituted for one with flowers if preferred. At each plate may be placed a spray of holly with its red berries. The ices may be served in little green and red baskets lined with waxed paper.

A sparkling snow effect is nice carried out in the dining-room and table decorations. The evergreen, holly and mistletoe used for decorations should be treated to a shower of thin gum arabic or alum water, and while still damp sprinkled with diamond dust, making the decorations look as if they were covered with hoarfrost or ice. Everything in the form of decoration should be white on the table except a touch of green and red which sprays of holly will provide. Use pure white china and white candle holders or crystal holders. Cover the white candles with white shades made of white frosted crepe paper which one may buy ready for use, and the edges may be decorated with tiny glass icicles. For a centerpiece for the table cut a circular mat out of cotton wadding, and in the center of this place a snowball made out of the same material. Sprinkle all over plentifully with diamond dust. On the top of the snowball place a spray of frosted holly, and partly encircle the ball with a diminutive Santa Claus, fur-clad and white-bearded, driving his eight reindeers attached to a tiny sled or sleigh containing little bundles done up in red and green paper. Have at each plate snowballs made out of frosted crepe paper and decorate the tops with sprays of frosted holly; if liked, these balls may contain souvenirs of the occasion or some little toy.

At each end of the table have a crystal dish

heaped up with popcorn balls; these are nice rolled in a sticky sirup, then rolled in rock candy that has been pounded into bits. These will sparkle in the light. Snowball cakes may be made by cutting any white loaf cake into ball shape, icing in white, and then rolling them in cocoanut. Mashed potatoes may be formed into snowballs and surrounded with parsley to give a touch of green. The ice-cream may be molded in the same shape also. The place-cards may be decorated with little frosted snow scenes, and also with a bit of holly.

A pretty table effect that is especially dainty is carried out in gold and white. The china and table linen should all be in pure white. Have for the centerpiece a gilded basket or gold bowl filled with pure white blossoms, such as carnations or roses. The place-cards should be gilt-edged and if liked a little figure in gold may be painted or appliqued on. Serve yellow bonbons in little white or gold receptacles.

Another pretty effect may be obtained with

gilt stars. Have a touch of green with this decoration; for instance, in the center of the table may be arranged a star made of evergreen, and in the center of this place a smaller gilt star. The place-cards may be decorated with a border of tiny gilt stars, or just one larger gilt star in the corner. White bonbon boxes decorated with tiny gilt stars are nice to have at each plate; and if candles are used, have them decorated with tiny stars.

CHRISTMAS DECORATIONS FOR CHILDREN'S TABLES

A Christmas-tree table always delights the children. Paint a pot red and plant in it a small Christmas tree. Choose a nice-shaped tree; just a branch of evergreen, if of the right shape and nicely trimmed, will serve the purpose very nicely. Be sure to have it firm and secure in the pot. It can be decorated with tinsel, cranberries, popcorn and tiny toys, stars and little stockings made of cambric or tarletan. Tiny candles can be used on the tree, and everything should be on the small order. Little individual trees to place at each plate can be made by taking small sprays of evergreen and sticking them in the ends of spools that have been painted or colored red. Fasten on the top of each tree a gilt star, a little Santa Claus or a tiny red candle.

A nice centerpiece for a children's table is made by laying a circular mat of fleecy cotton in the center of the table and sprinkling it well with mica. Place a wreath of holly around the edge, and coming across the snow have a little sleigh drawn by reindeers with Santa Claus driving, surrounded by his toys. Santa Claus in his aeroplane is another good idea. The aeroplane should be suspended over the table, and for a centerpiece have a row of little pasteboard houses arranged on a square of cotton. These houses can be made of red cardboard, with windows and doors outlined with chalk or with ink, and with little chimneys pasted on. They can be bought if preferred.

CHRISTMAS DINNER MENUS

Menu No. 1

Clear Soup   Wafers

Roast Goose with Potato Stuffing

Escalloped Onions   Sweet Potato Puff   Celery

Cole Slaw

Orange Bavarian Pudding   Fruit Cake

Mince Pie

Nuts   Raisins   Candies

Coffee

Menu No. 2

Oyster Soup   Crackers

Roast Turkey with Rice Dressing

Baked Apples and Cranberries   Creamed Carrots

Glazed Sweet Potatoes

Apple and Date Salad   Cheese Straws

English Plum Pudding

Lemon Pie

Grape Cream

Fruits   .   '   Christmas Bonbons

Menu No. 3

Tomato Bouillon   Croutons

Roast Duck with Mushroom Sauce

Sweet Potato Croquettes   Pea Patties

Jellied Tomato Salad   Cream Cheese Balls

Celery   Olives   Pickles

Steamed Date Pudding with Orange Sauce

Bonbons   Nuts

Coffee

SWEET POTATO PUFF

3 cupfuls sweet potatoes	3 eggs
½ cupful cream	Salt and pepper

Peel, wash and boil some sweet potatoes, and pass through a potato ricer, then season with the cream, salt and pepper, and add the well-beaten egg yolks. Beat up the whites of the eggs until stiff and fold in. Mix lightly, and put in a buttered bake-dish and bake until puffed up and a nice brown on top.

ORANGE BAVARIAN PUDDING

1 pint orange-juice	1 cupful rich cream
2 tablespoonfuls gelatin	½ cupful boiling water
½ cupful sugar	1 teaspoonful orange
½ cupful cold water	extract

Dissolve the gelatin in the cold water, then stir in the boiling water, add the sugar. When cool, stir in the cream beaten to a stiff froth. Beat up until light and foamy. Pour in wetted mold and chill. Turn out, and serve with whipped cream, and garnish with orange carpels.

BAKED APPLES AND CRANBERRIES

Sweet apples   Cranberries
Cinnamon   Sugar

Peel, halve and core some nice large sweet or semi-sweet apples, and fill the cavities with sugar and cinnamon mixed. Place these in the bottom of a bake-dish and place over them a layer of cranberries, sprinkled liberally with sugar. Bake in the oven until the apples are tender and the cranberry juice has penetrated them.

MUSHROOM SAUCE FOR ROAST DUCK

1 pint canned mushrooms   ½ cupful water
2 tablespoonfuls butter   2 tablespoonfuls flour
½ cupful milk   ½ cupful stock
½ teaspoonful salt   ¼ teaspoonful pepper

Make a cream sauce by blending together in a double boiler the butter and flour and the water, milk and soup stock. Stir until smooth and thick, then season to taste. Turn in the mushrooms and simmer slowly for ten or fifteen minutes. If too thick thin with a little milk or stock.

Pea Patties

To make these take small rolls and scoop out some of the centers from each and toast a delicate brown in the oven. Drain a can of peas from all liquid, and place in a colander and throw some cold water over them. Make a cream sauce with butter, flour and milk; season to taste, and stir in the peas. Fill these in the patty rolls. If preferred the peas may be served in pastry patty shells.

Steamed Date Pudding

1 cupful stoned and chopped dates	1 teaspoonful salt
2 tablespoonfuls grated orange peel	1 cupful sweet milk
¾ cupful sugar	2 level cupfuls bread
1 cupful flour	2 teaspoonfuls baking-powder
	1 well-beaten egg

Sift the baking-powder and salt with the flour and mix it and the other ingredients thoroughly together. Pour into a greased mold, and steam for two hours at least. Serve with an orange sauce made the same as lemon sauce only use orange-juice and orange extract for flavoring instead of the lemon.

II

HOSPITALITY FOR SPECIAL DAYS

CHAPTER II

HOSPITALITY FOR SPECIAL DAYS

TABLE DECORATIONS FOR ST. VALENTINE'S DAY

HEARTS always make the most appropriate decorations for the St. Valentine's Day tables. A charming effect is obtained by cutting hearts out of crepe paper in all colors ranging from the palest pink to the deepest red. Place four red hearts in the center of the table, having the bottom of the hearts pointing towards the corners of the tables; then gradually arrange the hearts in a line from these, shading towards the pale pink hearts at the corners of the table. The hearts would be nice if cut in different sizes, the largest hearts placed in the center of the table and gradually smaller as they near the corners of the table. In the center of the table may be placed a vase or basket of pink or red roses. The place-cards may be pale pink, Valentine hearts.

A heart-shaped Jack Horner pie always makes a good centerpiece. Use a heart-shaped pasteboard box foundation for this pie. Cover with pink crepe paper and pink paper roses; or with white crepe paper decorated with red heart pasters. From a hole in the center have ribbons extend to each plate. Have the ribbons in the pie attached to little candy motto hearts; these may be pulled out at the close of the luncheon. At each plate may be a heart-shaped frame holding the picture of a pretty girl's head or of a Cupid. Letter the names at the bottom of these, and they will serve as place-cards. If you wish something simpler try this: Place in the center of the table a red lace paper mat in heart shape. In the center of this place a pink-covered pasteboard box, somewhat smaller than the mat. Paste a white heart in the center of the cover an inch or two smaller than the cover of the box, and in the center of this paste a small red heart. Have smaller heart-shaped boxes to match at each plate to hold the heart-shaped bon-bons.

St. Valentine's Day Luncheons

Heart Menus

Menu No. 1

Cream Soup with Pimiento Hearts

Cheese and Nut Hearts

Salmon Croquettes   Ham Canapes

Tomato Heart Salad

Sweethearts

Ice-Cream Hearts   Cupid Cakes

Heart-shaped Bonbons

Menu No. 2

Tomato Bisque

Pimiento and Cheese Sandwiches   Lobster Hearts

Beet Heart Salad

Heart Tarts

Heart's Delight   Angel Hearts

Macaroon Hearts

In preparing the heart-shaped dishes for the heart menus you will need heart-shaped cutters in various sizes. If you cannot find the sizes desired at the tin store, a tinsmith can make them in any size you may wish. You will also need heart-shaped molds and heart-shaped patty-pans.

CHEESE AND NUT HEARTS

2 cupfuls flour
1 teaspoonful baking-
powder
½ teaspoonful salt

1 cupful pecan nut-meats
½ cupful cream cheese
1 egg and a little ice-water

Sift the flour, baking-powder and salt thoroughly together, add the pecan nut-meats chopped fine, and just enough ice-water to make a dough that will roll out nicely. Roll out about an eighth of an inch thick on a floured board, and spread with the cream cheese. Fold over three or four times, roll in thin sheets and cut out with a heart-shaped cutter. Brush over each heart with the white of an egg, and bake a delicate brown in the oven. These are nice served with the cream soup or bouillon with little beet hearts or pimiento hearts floating in it.

CHEESE SANDWICHES IN HEART-SHAPE

1 cupful cream cheese
1 teaspoonful paprika
Pimientoes

1 teaspoonful salt
¼ cupful butter
Bread

Cut the bread in thin slices. Mix into a

paste the cream cheese, butter, salt and paprika, and spread on one-half of the bread hearts. With a smaller heart-cutter cut out openings in the other half of the bread hearts. Place on top of the other pieces and fill the heart openings with chopped pimientoes. The effect of a red heart within a white one is very pretty.

LOBSTER HEARTS

1 teaspoonful lemon-juice	1 can lobster
2 tablespoonfuls butter	3 tablespoonfuls flour
1 egg	Pie pastry
1 pint milk	

Bake a rich baking-powder pie pastry and roll a fourth of an inch thick. Cut about a third of the dough into thick narrow strips. Cut the rest out with a heart-shaped cutter, and place the strips around the edge of each to form a deep cup-like edge. Drain the liquor from the lobster into a bowl and free from bones. Pour over the lobster a white sauce made by blending together in a double boiler the butter and flour. Heat the milk and stir in, and also the liquor from about the lobster. Stir constantly until smooth, and season. Fill the pastry shells with this mixture and bake in a moderate oven about twenty minutes. Brush the inside of the shells with the white of an egg before placing in the lobster mixture.

HEART TARTS

Pie pastry   Strawberry preserves

Line heart-shaped patty pans with good pie pastry and bake a delicate brown in the oven. When cool, fill with strawberry preserves.

ANGEL HEARTS

Angel cake   Candied cherries
Pink fondant

Take an angel cake that is a day or so old and cut into slices about half an inch thick; then cut out with a small heart-shaped cutter. Dip each little heart into pink fondant and decorate with tiny hearts cut out of candied cherries.

HEART'S DELIGHT

½ cupful water	1 cupful sugar
1 cupful cream	2 oz. gelatin or jelly powder
1 pint cherry-juice	Candied cherries

Soak two ounces of gelatin or required amount of jelly powder until soft; dissolve by adding one-half cupful of boiling water. Add to this the red cherry juice and the sugar. If the juice has already been sweetened use only a half cupful of sugar. Stir until it begins to grow thick; then fold in the cream, beat until stiff. Line heart molds with little candied cherry hearts and pour in the mixture. Let stand until firm and turn out.

TABLE DECORATIONS FOR ST. PATRICK'S DAY

The color scheme should be white and green. Have as many foliage plants and vines about the dining-room as possible. With these may be used white jonquils, snowdrops, narcissi and crocuses, also white tulips.

For a centerpiece a basket or pot of oxalis would be pretty and appropriate, as it comes nearer to the shamrock than anything else; if you do not have the oxalis, then a pretty effect may be obtained with ferns and white spring blossoms. Arrange a mat in the center of the table of the delicate asparagus plumosa or maiden-hair ferns. In the center of this place a pretty rustic or fancy basket filled with ferns and white blossoms. If preferred, a green or white bowl may be used instead of the basket. A cluster of green and white carnations in a crystal vase on a green mat is also effective. Green candlesticks with white shades will add to the general effect. Place-cards should be decorated with shamrocks done in water colors or appliqued on. Small green silk flags with a golden harp outlined on them can be crossed and fastened to the white cloth at intervals. Small green baskets filled with white mints may be placed at each plate. White china decorated with green would add to the appearance of the table, or pure white china may be used.

ST. PATRICK'S DAY LUNCHEONS

Menu No. 1

Cream of Spinach Soup   Pistachio Nut Wafers
Baked Asparagus with Hollandaise Sauce
Jellied Chicken Salad
Celery Rolls
Mint Ice   Erin Loaf Cake
St. Patrick's Candies

Menu No. 2

Cream of Pea Soup
Dublin Salad   Lettuce Sandwiches
Fish with Spinach Sauce
Pickles   Olives
Pistachio Ice-Cream   Blarney Stones
Emerald Sea Foam

CREAM OF SPINACH SOUP

2 cupfuls boiled spinach	1 quart milk
2 tablespoonfuls flour	Slice of onion
2 tablespoonfuls butter	Salt and pepper

Place the milk in a double boiler and add the onion, and bring to a boil, then remove the onion. Blend the flour and butter together, then gradually stir in the scalded milk. Add the cooked spinach, which should be passed through a sieve. Stir until thoroughly mixed, then season with salt and pepper. Serve in bouillon cups with a dot of whipped cream in the center.

PISTACHIO NUT TARTS OR WAFERS

Pie pastry
2 eggs
½ cupful pistachio nuts

3 tablespoonfuls powdered sugar

Make a short pie pastry. Mix a tablespoonful of the powdered sugar with the flour on the board, and roll out very thin. Dip fancy cutters in flour, and cut out; then pierce half of the cakes with a small circular cutter. Some of the cakes can be made with one hole, some with two or three. Place these on greased pans and bake in the oven a pale brown. Make a paste with the stiffly beaten whites of the eggs, the powdered sugar and the nut-meats chopped very fine. Spread this on the cakes left whole, and then place the cakes with the holes on top. If there is any of the paste left fill into the holes. If you are making many cakes, double the amount of nuts and egg-whites, so you will have enough for all.

BAKED ASPARAGUS

1 pint asparagus tips	2 tablespoonfuls butter
Salt and pepper	Bread-crumbs

Use only the tender tips, and place in a baking-dish. Dot over with the butter, and season with salt and pepper. Cover with buttered crumbs, seasoned with a little lemon-juice, or sauce. Bake in the oven until the crumbs are brown. Serve with a Hollandaise cream sauce or a plain cream sauce, as liked.

Sauce Hollandaise.—Place in a double boiler one-half cupful of butter that has been beaten to a cream, stir in the well-beaten yolks of four eggs. Beat up until thick and creamy, then add one-half teaspoonful of salt and the juice of half a lemon. Place over the fire and add gradually one cupful of hot water. Stir until thick and smooth. If this sauce is used with the asparagus do not add lemon to the crumbs.

CELERY ROLLS

Use small rolls, and one for each person to be served. Carefully remove some of the inside from each roll. Place in each cavity a teaspoonful of melted butter, distributing it over the sides. Chop some inside tender stalks of celery fine, season well with salt and pepper. Add a little chopped chicken or ham, and fill into the rolls. The meat can be omitted if liked.

ERIN LOAF CAKE

1 cupful butter	6 eggs
2 cupfuls of sugar	1 cupful of milk
3½ cupfuls of flour	1 teaspoonful almond
2 teaspoonfuls of baking-	extract
powder	Angelica

Cream together the butter and sugar, then add the milk and flour into which the baking-powder can be sifted, then fold in the stiffly beaten whites of the six eggs. Remove one-third of the batter and color with a few drops of green vegetable coloring. Pour some of the batter into a deep cake pan, then place over it a few spoonfuls of the green batter, then more of the white, and so on until all the batter is used. This will give a green and white effect. Ice the cake with white icing flavored with almond extract, and decorate with angelica in form of green leaves of the shamrock.

BLARNEY STONES

1 cupful of sugar
½ cupful of butter
1½ cupfuls of flour
1 cupful chopped walnut-
   meats
1 cupful chopped raisins
½ cupful sour milk

2 eggs
1 teaspoonful cinnamon
¼ teaspoonful cloves
¼ teaspoonful nutmeg
1 teaspoonful soda
1 teaspoonful vanilla

Mix together the dry ingredients. Cream together the sugar and butter, add the eggs, milk and vanilla, stir into the dry ingredients and beat thoroughly. This should make a stiff drop batter; if not, add a little more flour. Drop by spoonfuls onto a greased pan, and bake a nice brown.

CREAM OF PEA SOUP

1 pint cooked peas	1 cupful cooked lettuce
¼ cupful almonds	3 cupfuls milk
1 cupful cream	2 tablespoonfuls flour
2 tablespoonfuls butter	1 teaspoonful salt
¼ teaspoonful pepper	1 teaspoonful sugar

Blend together in a double boiler the butter and the flour, and add one cupful of milk, stirring constantly until smooth and thick; season with the salt, sugar and pepper; then stir in the remainder of the milk. Pass the peas and the lettuce through a sieve and add this purée to the milk. Bring to the boil, then stir in the cupful of cream and finely chopped almonds.

SPINACH SAUCE FOR BAKED FISH

2 tablespoonfuls butter	Salt
2 tablespoonfuls flour	1 cupful milk
½ cupful spinach-juice	1 tablespoonful lemon-juice

Place the butter and flour together in a double boiler and blend thoroughly, then gradually add the milk, and stir until smooth and thick. Stir in the thick spinach-juice, and season to taste with salt and pepper; then add the lemon-juice. If this does not make the sauce a nice green, add a little vegetable coloring in addition to the spinach juice.

MINT ICE

3 oranges	1 quart cold water
3 lemons	Mint leaves
Essence of peppermint	2 cupfuls sugar
1 tablespoonful gelatin	2 egg-whites

Simmer together the water, the rind of two lemons and a handful of mint leaves and the sugar. When it begins to thicken into a sirup remove the leaves and rind and add the gelatin that has been dissolved in one-half cupful cold water; add the juice of the oranges and the lemons, and the essence of peppermint, using a few drops. Color a deep green with green vegetable coloring. Pour into ice-cream freezer and freeze until mushy; then add the stiffly beaten whites of the eggs. Pack down in salt and ice, and let stand two or three hours.

Pistachio Ice-cream

1 cupful pistachio nuts	2 quarts cream
½ cupful almonds	1 pound sugar
1 teaspoonful pistachio extract	½ teaspoonful almond extract

Add the sugar to a pint of the cream and bring to the boil. Set aside to cool, then add the remainder of the cream, the extracts, and one-fourth teaspoonful salt. Pour into a freezer, and when partly frozen add the chopped nut-meats. Complete the freezing; then let stand an hour or so to ripen up. If liked this may be colored a pale green with vegetable coloring.

TABLE DECORATIONS FOR EASTERTIDE

Floral Decorations for the Easter Table

Flowers have always held an important place in the celebration of the Easter festival, and the spring blossoms, such as violets, narcissi, jonquils, hyacinths, tulips, daffodils, primroses, valley lilies, pansies, and sweet peas forced for the occasion, all make delightful table decorations.

At no season is there a better opportunity to show one's artistic skill and taste than at this season, when there is such a wealth of material to choose from. The regular Easter lilies are often objected to for table decoration on account of the strong perfume; in this case calla lilies will nicely take their place. Some delightful color schemes may be carried out with the spring blossoms in the Easter colors, which are yellow, the color of sunlight; pale green, the color of spring; white, the symbol of purity, and "there are some purple for Passiontide" also.

If the table decorations are to be calla lilies, then use for a centerpiece a large bouquet of these pure white blossoms, and fill their waxen cups with tiny bunches of the dainty blue forget-me-nots, bluets, or violets. Have a single lily at each plate, and also have the cups of these filled with the small blue blossoms. The place-cards should be cut out of white or cream celluloid in shape of calla lilies painted in the center with forget-me-nots.

A pretty scheme may be entirely carried out

in white calla lilies. Fill a crystal vase with the lilies and use as a centerpiece, and at each plate have a single calla lily with a bit of silver gauze tied to the stem. If candlesticks are used, have the candlesticks of silver or crystal, with silvered paper shades.

If the decorations for the table are to be Easter lilies, the following scheme may be carried out: Fill a tall crystal vase with a dozen or more of the lilies, and place on a circular mirror. Wreathe the edge with vines, and any small spring blossoms. The place-cards may be lilies cut out of water-color paper or celluloid of ivory tint; have a single blossom and one or two leaves. Outline the flower to bring out the petals; then shade them with cream and pale green water-color paints. The stamens should be painted brown, tipped with yellow, and the stems and leaves dark green. Letter or write the guests' names on the leaves with gold ink. Place one of these lilies at each plate. For bonbon boxes use small round or hexagon-shaped boxes; if not readily procured they may be easily made.

Cover the box with pale green paper, also line the box with crepe paper, using white paper. Cut a lily out of ivory-tinted water-color paper. Outline the petals with gold and shade a dull green, paint the stamens and pistils brown tipped with yellow. Fasten the lily to the cover of the box so that the ends of the petals will extend over the edge of the box. Fill the boxes made after this manner with bonbons and place one at each plate.

EASTER EGG-SHELL DECORATIONS

Egg-shells alone, prosaic though they may sound, can be depended upon to furnish exceedingly pretty decorative effects; and egg-shells, after the Easter cake-baking and dessert-making are accomplished, are apt to be a drug in the home market. Care needs to be taken, of course, in emptying the shells of their contents, to keep the shell intact. For a centerpiece get a tiny evergreen tree, or—better still—a little shrub or branches of the blossoming forsythia or flowering currant. Decorate this with shining gilt stars and crosses, and from the branches hang egg-shells—hen or duck—that have been decorated in oil or water colors. Some may have painted on them little landscapes, suggestive of the springtime, others flowers appropriate to the season, or flights of butterflies.

These shells can be left in their natural colors for a background or be solidly colored before applying the decorations. If no one in the family is clever with the brush, some of the shells may be gilded and others colored blue, with gilt stars, butterflies, and birds cut from cards or paper and pasted on, the edges being touched up with gilt. Run baby ribbon in delicate shades through the holes at either end of each shell from which the contents were blown out, tie the ends of the ribbons together in perky little bows and suspend. These may be distributed afterwards as souvenirs.

To make name cards, mount egg-shells, with faces and hair painted on them, on the ends of plain cards, writing the name at the other end. Strips of cardboard or stiff paper in a circle can be used for the necks, and they should be glued to the small end of the shell. The head at each place should suggest, in some way, the characteristics of the guest. For instance, the acknowledged belle of the crowd should have an exceedingly pretty face, with a pink or blue crepe paper frill about the neck and a picture hat of crepe paper on the head. For a quiet person, a Quaker or Quakeress with Quaker hat or bonnet; for the student, a college cap, or mortar-board.

CHILDREN'S EASTER TABLES

Unique and delightful table decorations for the children's Easter tables are easily carried out. A novel and pleasing centerpiece for the table may be made by taking a tray, filling it with sand and concealing the edge with smilax or ferns. A little fence made of water-color paper or pasteboard painted to resemble wood may be placed around the edge of the tray; this makes a good chicken yard. Make a good coop also of pasteboard or cardboard, and place in the center of the yard. Buy a toy hen with a brood of tiny, downy chicks and also a rooster. Place the rooster on top of the coop, the hen inside the coop, and the chicks in the yard. Take a little toy dish and fill with cornmeal, and a little toy tin-pan of water, and place near the coop. At each plate may be little nests of candy eggs.

A bunny centerpiece is also appropriate. A coach may be fashioned out of a grapefruit rind, with wheels made of the slices of lemon. To this can be harnessed six little bunnies, using narrow ribbon for harness. At each plate may be little toy bunnies bearing tiny baskets of eggs on their backs. A cake iced with maple or chocolate icing, and decorated with marshmallow bunnies also makes a nice centerpiece.

EASTER MENUS FOR CHILDREN
Orange Pulp in Orange Shell Baskets
Rice Croquettes in Egg-shape   Egg Sandwiches
Cream Cheese Eggs in Nests of Cress
Ice-Cream (in form of chicks)
Egg-shaped Sponge Cakes
Egg Candies

Cream of Corn Soup
Creamed Whitefish in Egg-shaped Ramekins
Peanut Sandwiches
Boiled and Colored Eggs
Mashed Potatoes (molded in egg-shape in parsley baskets)
Ice-Cream (egg-shape)   Little Cakes
Egg-shaped Bonbons

Bunny Sandwiches   Carrot Eggs in Cream Sauce
Cream Cheese (molded in form of rabbits with clove eyes)
Easter Omelet
Ice-Cream Bunnies   Bunny Cakes
Marshmallow Bunnies

Fruit Mixture in Lemon Shells
Chicken Sandwiches   Potato Chick Croquettes
Creamed Asparagus
Custards or Easter Egg Dessert   Sunshine Cake
Easter Candies

POTATO CHICKS

Cold mashed potatoes   Cream
Butter   Egg-white
Celery leaves   Almonds

Beat the mashed potatoes up until light, adding a little cream and butter. Mold quickly into the shape of chicks. Glaze over the outside with the white of egg, and place in the oven a few moments. Halved, blanched almonds may be stuck in for the beaks, cloves for the eyes, and celery leaves for the wings and the tails, and you have yellow chicks which will look nice standing in a nest of cress or parsley.

EASTER EGG DESSERT

1 quart good milk	1 cupful sugar
4 tablespoonfuls corn-starch	1 cupful water
	½ teaspoonful salt
2 tablespoonfuls vanilla	1 ounce chocolate
1 egg	Red coloring
Lemon jelly	Whipped cream

Heat the milk in a double boiler with the sugar and then stir in the corn-starch dissolved in the water (milk may be used). Stir until smooth and thick, season with salt and vanilla. Divide the mixture into four portions. Leave one portion whites, stir into another the beaten yolk of egg, in another the chocolate, melted, and in the other a little red fruit coloring. Have ready as many egg-shells as you have guests. Rinse out and stand on end in pan of salt or sawdust. Fill with the blanc-mange, and place in a cool place until cold.

EASTER DINNER MENUS

Consommé   Wafers

Salmon Loaf with Tomato Sauce

Roast Chicken or Veal

Spiced Pears   Celery

Escalloped Eggs and Celery

Creamed Cauliflower

Grapefruit Salad   Rolls

Pineapple-Orange Sherbet

Sunshine Cake   Salted Almonds

Pimiento Canapes

Mushroom Soup   Crackers

Baked Whitefish with Lemon Sauce

Mixed Pickles

Crown of Lamb   Cherry Mint Sauce

Mint Glazed Carrots   Potato Rissolées

Easter Salad   Rolls

Ginger Ice Cream

Orange Cake   Nut Macaroons

Crackers   Cheese

Mints

GRAPEFRUIT SALAD

3 grapefruits	3 oranges
Pineapple	Lemon sirup dressing

Cut the grapefruits in halves and remove the pulp carefully so as to leave the cups perfect. Remove the seeds from the pulp and shred. Peel and shred the oranges, and cut up the pineapple into bits. Mix thoroughly together, and fill into the grapefruit cups. Make a lemon sirup dressing with one cupful sugar, one cupful lemon-juice, adding a little of the rind. Boil to a thick sirup. Pour over the fruit mixture and chill before serving.

PINEAPPLE-ORANGE SHERBET

1 can grated pineapple	2 cupfuls sugar
1 cupful orange juice	2 lemons
1 quart water	1 tablespoonful gelatin
1 teaspoonful lemon extract	2 egg-whites

Boil the sugar and water together until a thin sirup, add the gelatin dissolved in a little cold water; when cold, add the lemon and orange juice and the flavoring. Strain through a coarse cheese-cloth. Pour into freezer and partly freeze; then stir in the grated pineapple and the beaten egg-whites and finish freezing.

CHOCOLATE CUSTARD

1 pint rich milk	4 eggs
½ cupful sugar	1 tablespoonful gelatin
1 teaspoonful vanilla	2 ounces baker's chocolate
Pinch of salt	

Beat up the yolks of the eggs, add the sugar; then pour over them the scalded milk, stirring constantly. Cook until it thickens; then add the gelatin that has been dissolved in a little cold water. Let this partly cool, then stir in the vanilla and the melted chocolate. Fold in the stiffly beaten whites of the eggs. Beat up until light and foamy. Pour into a mold or molds. When firm and cold turn out and serve with whipped cream.

POTATO CROQUETTES

6 medium-sized potatoes	1 tablespoonful butter
3 eggs	Salt and pepper
Bread-crumbs	Spinach

Peel, wash and boil the potatoes until tender, adding a half teaspoonful of salt to the water.

Drain, and pass through a potato ricer. Mix the melted butter and two well-beaten eggs into the potato, season with salt and pepper to taste. Form the potato mixture into egg-shape, then roll in bread-crumbs and fry a delicate brown in deep, hot fat. By adding one-fourth cupful of spinach to the potatoes you will have pale green croquettes.

ESCALLOPED EGGS AND CELERY

2 heads of celery	6 eggs
2 tablespoonfuls flour	2 cupfuls milk
2 tablespoonfuls butter	Salt and pepper
Bread-crumbs	

Boil the eggs in their shells until hard. Clean and cut the celery into inch lengths and boil in slightly salted water until tender. Make a cream sauce with the butter, flour and milk, and season with salt and pepper to taste. Place the chopped eggs, celery and cream sauce in alternate layers in a bake-dish, having the last layer of the sauce. Cover with buttered bread-crumbs and bake in a moderate oven until brown on top.

SALMON LOAF WITH TOMATO SAUCE

1 can salmon	3 tablespoonfuls of butter
3 eggs	1 cupful of bread-crumbs
Salt and pepper	Tomato sauce

Remove the oil, skin and bones from one can of salmon and pick into bits. Cream the butter and beat the egg well and add to the bread-crumbs; then add the butter and the salmon and season with salt and pepper. Beat all together and steam one hour in a buttered mold, or it can be baked in the oven in a covered pan. Make a tomato sauce with one tablespoonful each of flour, butter, and add one cupful tomato juice and season. Place the loaf on hot plate and pour the sauce over it.

MINT-GLAZED CARROTS

Carrots	Sugar
Butter	Mint leaves

Wash and scrape as many medium-sized carrots as there are persons to be served and cut into thin slices. Boil them in slightly salted water fifteen minutes, then drain well. Place the slices in a saucepan and add to each half-dozen carrots used two-thirds cupful each of sugar and butter and one tablespoonful of mint-leaves, minced. Cook until the carrots are well glazed and nice and tender. These are nice served with a border of green peas.

POTATO RISSOLÉES

New potatoes	Cream sauce
Deep fat	Salt and pepper

Wash the potatoes, peel, and cut into egg-shape, using a sharp knife. Place in cold water for twenty minutes, then remove and drain. Place in the oven and bake until partly cooked; then fry a delicate brown in deep hot fat. Serve with a cream sauce and garnish with parsley.

SPONGE-CAKE EGGS

Bake a sponge-cake, using any good sponge-cake batter. When cold, cut in egg-shape and ice with yellow icing; or the sponge-cake batter may be poured into egg-shells from which the contents have been removed from one end.

Clean thoroughly and oil with a little melted butter. Place in a pan of salt so they will be held upright; then fill about two-thirds full, and bake in a quick oven.

EASTER CAKE

Make a good loaf cake by following a loaf-cake recipe given, or any reliable recipe. When baked, cover thickly with white icing. On the top of the cake arrange little nests formed from strips of citron or orange peel. Fill the nests with small candy eggs, or decorate the cake with candied violets, or candy chicks, as liked.

TABLE DECORATIONS FOR MAY DAY

May luncheons are particularly popular since the month of May offers such a wealth of materials and possibilities for table decorations. Flowers and ferns supply never-ending resources; they are so suggestive of spring-time loveliness that it is a delight to arrange

them for table decorations. A delightful table
can be had by placing in the center of the table
a May-pole two or three feet high; this can be
made of a broomstick cut the desired length,
with standards nailed on one end for supports.
Wind this around with green ribbon, then decorate freely with daisies, and heap daisies at
the foot or base of the pole until the standards
are concealed.

Have a ring fastened in the pole at the top,
and from this have daisy chains extending to
each plate, ending in tiny May-baskets filled
with daisies and ferns. Paste a row of daisies
flat across the top of the place-cards or thrust
a single daisy through a slit in one corner.
White, yellow and green should be the colors
used in all appointments and courses served
with this table scheme. White china with gold
bands would be nice or white china decorated
with a delicate green.

Another pretty idea for a May-pole luncheon
is to wind the pole with green ribbon, heap
moss and ferns at the base, and have a light
basket of ferns and flowers on the top of the

pole. Vines should be trained around the pole
as if growing. Have a chain of smilax reaching to each plate or to each corner of the table.
These can end in little May-poles entwined
with ribbon and smilax, with a tiny May-bas-
ket on top of each filled with flowers. It
would be nice to have strands of different
kinds of flowers, ending in a basket of the
same kind as the chain; as for one a strand of
violets ending in a basket of violets, one pansies, one valley lilies and so on. Artificial
flowers can be used in making the strands but
real flowers should be used in the baskets.
The favors may be little flower-shaped booklets, containing quotations on each guest's
particular flower; for instance, the daisy booklet contains daisy quotations, the pansy book
pansy quotations, and so on.

Decorations for a May-basket Luncheon

The table will present a charming picture if
decorated in the following manner: Procure a
number of small cheap baskets—they may be

procured from a five-and-ten-cent store. En-
amel them in white, and the delicate shades of
pink, blue, green, lavender, and yellow, also
gild and silver a few of them. The baskets
should be filled with small spring blossoms,
the different flowers harmonizing with the baskets in which they are arranged. For instance,
the white blossoms should be in the blue baskets, or in the pink or lavender baskets; while
the blue blossoms will prove very effective
arranged in the cream, yellow or gilt baskets,
or the silvered ones.

The pink and red blossoms will look well in
the pale green, gray, white and silvered baskets. These baskets should be placed at the
plates. Over the center of the table suspend
a large hoop, which should be first covered
with green cloth, then with vines and ferns,
with a blossom worked in at intervals. Suspend this hoop from the ceiling or lights by
means of four vine-covered ropes. All around
the hoop hang tiny May-baskets filled with
small spring blossoms. From this hoop may
be stretched streamers of ribbon or flowers to

the baskets at the plates. Tie to the handles of the baskets.

MENUS FOR MAY DAY LUNCHEONS

Yellow, White and Green Menu

Marguerites   Marguerite Salad
Asparagus with Yellow Sauce
Olives   Cream Cheese-Parsley Balls
Ice-Cream with Green Mint Cherries
Yellow and White Bonbons   Lemon Cake

Pink and White Menu

Cream of Shrimp Soup   Pimiento Sandwiches
Sweetbreads in Pink Cream Sauce   Pink Beet Salad
Pink and White Radishes
Pink and White Ice-Cream   May-pole Cakes

MARGUERITES

1 dozen round wafers	½ cupful powdered sugar
1 tablespoonful cream	1 teaspoonful vanilla
¼ cupful chopped nut-meats	1 egg-white
Blanched almonds	1 tablespoonful orange-peel

Beat the egg-white stiff, and stir in the powdered sugar, cream, candied orange-peel chopped very fine, and the finely chopped nut-meats. Spread over the wafers. Decorate the top with marguerites formed of halves of lightly blanched almonds to represent the petals, with a bit of candied orange-peel for the centers.

MARGUERITE SALAD

Tomato jelly	Hard-boiled eggs
Mayonnaise dressing	Salt and pepper

Make some tomato jelly, and mold in shallow molds. Chill, and when cold, turn out on lettuce leaves arranged on individual plates. Cut the hard-boiled eggs in halves, then in lengthwise strips, and arrange the whites on the jelly for petals of the flower. Work into the egg-yolks the seasoning and a little mayonnaise. Place this in the center of the flower.

CREAM CHEESE PARSLEY BALLS

To make these, take some good cream cheese, and mix into it a tablespoonful of cream and one tablespoonful of finely chopped parsley. Form into balls, and serve in nest of parsley.

PIMIENTO SANDWICHES

1 small can pimientoes	1 dozen olives
1 cupful cream cheese	Mayonnaise dressing
Salt and pepper	Bread and butter

Chop the pimientoes and work into the cheese, also the olives chopped fine. Season with salt, pepper and mayonnaise or boiled dressing. Use as a filling between thin slices of buttered bread.

SWEETBREADS WITH PINK SAUCE

1 pair sweetbreads	Cream sauce
Red vegetable coloring	Toast or pastry shells

Cut the sweetbreads into small pieces after they have been parboiled and cooled. Make a cream sauce with one tablespoonful each of flour and butter, and one cupful scalded milk; stir until smooth, and season with salt and paprika, and color with a little red vegetable coloring to a nice pink. Place the sweetbread in this, and heat thoroughly. Serve on rounds of delicately toasted bread or in pastry shells.

TABLE DECORATIONS FOR
HALLOWE'EN

The table decoration for a nut luncheon should be carried out, partly at least, with nuts. A simple, effective centerpiece is made by filling a basket with mixed nuts, and placing it on a mat of red autumn leaves. Twine the handles and edge of the basket with native vines, such as the bittersweet bearing bright berries. A nut cake would also make an unusual centerpiece. Follow any good hickory nut recipe, ice in white and decorate with halves of English walnut shells. Set the cake on a mat of bright sumach, or other bright autumn leaves, or wreathe it with chrysanthemums. To decorate the walnut shells remove the inside, wash the shells, and when dry outline brownie faces on them. Place them around the sides of the cake in a row and above their brownie heads make melted chocolate caps. Paint the chocolate on with a brush or with the fingers. This will not spoil the cake, as the shells will slip off easily when you wish to cut it.

For place-cards put fortune verses in the halves of English walnut shells, outlining brownie faces on the outside. Glue these shells to the top of correspondence cards. Cut out brownie bodies from brown paper and paste below, or a body may be outlined on the card. A half-cone of brown paper can be pasted on top of the brownie head for a cap. Below this nut brownie letter these words, " I've an idea in my head for you." The name of the guest should be lettered on the top or the bottom of the card. Have at each plate a small fancy basket or box in dull red filled with nut and chocolate candies. If you wish something more elaborate you can string cranberries and peanuts alternately and entwine around the principal dishes, or bring them down from the chandelier to each plate and fasten to the handles of the little baskets holding the bon-bons.

APPLE LUNCHEON

If apple dishes have a prominent place on the menu apples should also form the centerpiece. Polish red apples until they shine and heap up in a fancy dish or basket with them. If you like you may arrange a row of green or purple grapes around the edge.

For a comic decoration paste on the side of each apple, eyes, nose and mouth cut out of white, gold or any light-colored paper, if the apples are red. If the apples are green or white then use black or some dark colored paper; or if preferred, little Jack-o'-lantern faces can be bought and one pasted on the four sides of each apple. Apple cases in which salads, frappé and sherbets are served can also be decorated in this manner.

MENUS FOR HALLOWE'EN LUNCHEONS

Nut Menu

Cream of Chestnut Soup

Oyster Patties   Nut Sandwiches

Apple-nut Salad

Grape Sherbet   Nut Cake

Nut Bonbons

Candied Chestnuts   Salted Almonds

Apple Menu

Cream of Carrot Soup
Brown and White Bread and Butter Sandwiches
Stuffed Baked Apples   Creamed Chicken
Waldorf Salad
Apple Frappé in Apple Cases   Apple Sauce Cake

CREAM OF CHESTNUT SOUP

1 quart chestnuts	3 cupfuls water
1 pint white stock	1 pint thin cream sauce
1 tablespoonful butter	1 tablespoonful flour
1 teaspoonful parsley	1 teaspoonful salt
¼ teaspoonful pepper	½ teaspoonful sugar

Select nice large chestnuts and boil in water that has been slightly salted for about thirty minutes; then remove the brown skins and place in the three cupfuls of water and boil for at least another half hour. Make a thin cream sauce with the flour, butter and one cupful of milk and one cupful of cream. Season. Pass the chestnuts through a sieve, add to this the stock and the cream sauce. Simmer slowly for ten or fifteen minutes and add more seasoning if necessary. Serve in bouillon cups with a tea-spoonful of whipped cream on top of each cup.

OYSTER PATTIES

Puff pastry
2 tablespoonfuls butter
1 pint oysters
1 tablespoonful lemon-
   juice

1 pint good milk
2 tablespoonfuls flour
Salt, pepper
A few drops of onion-
   juice

Prepare a good puff pastry and bake in patty-pans or shallow gem pans. Make a thick white sauce with the flour, butter and milk. Instead of using all milk you can use one cupful cream and one cupful stock, season to taste. Drain the oysters of all juice before measuring, add to the sauce and boil two or three minutes. Serve in the patty shells.

STUFFED BAKED APPLES

Tart apples
1 cupful nut-meats
1 teaspoonful cinnamon

1 cupful raisins
½ cupful brown sugar
½ teaspoonful salt

Chop the nut-meats quite fine, also chop the raisins and mix together, add the brown sugar and the cinnamon, stirring until thoroughly blended. Cut a slice off the stem end of tart apples, and remove the cores, and part of the apple. Fill the cavities with the raisin and nut mixture, and bake in the oven until tender.

WALDORF SALAD

2 cupfuls chopped apple	1 cupful nut-meats
1 cupful mayonnaise dressing	Apple cups

Peel and core tart apples, and cut up into bits, add the chopped nut-meats and dress with the mayonnaise, then fill into apple cups made by carefully removing all the apple except a bit around the skin, just enough to keep the cups in shape. Sprinkle the inside with lemon juice to keep from getting a dark color.

HALLOWE'EN SUPPER MENUS

Menu No. 1

Oyster Sandwiches   Tomato Celery Salad

Individual Pumpkin Pies

Stuffed Pears   Sponge Cakes

Boiled Chestnuts

Menu No. 2

Mixed Sandwiches   Chicken Salad

Scalloped Potatoes
Pickles

Quince Loaf   Nut Cakes

Coffee

Menu No. 3

Nut Sandwiches   Shaved Ham

Molded Vegetable Salad

Peanut Ice-Cream   Fortune Wheels

Popcorn Fudge

Menu No. 4

Brownie Sandwiches   Goblin Salad

Fairies' Delight   Night-owl Cakes   ·

Jack-o'-lanterns

Hallowe'en Favorite

III

COMPANY LUNCHEONS IN VARI-ETY FOR ALL SEASONS

CHAPTER III

COMPANY LUNCHEONS IN VARIETY FOR ALL SEASONS

THERE is no more delightful way in which to entertain one's friends than by giving a luncheon or series of luncheons. These may be formal or informal affairs. The decorations and menu for an informal luncheon may be very simple, and need not require much work, and is an inexpensive way to entertain. If the luncheon is to be a formal one the decorations of the table and the menu may be as elaborate as one may wish to have them.

Whether informal or formal, luncheons may be made most delightful affairs. Charming and effective color schemes may be carried out both in the table decorations and in the menu. The spring and summertime of the year is an ideal time to give a luncheon or series of luncheons, since flowers always give a dainty yet festive appearance to the table, and one may carry out many pretty schemes with them with little expense. We give in this book a number of color schemes that are easily carried out.

Yellow and White

Grapefruit Cup Topped with White Grapes
Daisy Canapes   Potato Croquettes with Cream Sauce
Lily Salad   Orange Rollovers
Spring Delight   Sunshine and Angel Cakes
Yellow and White Bonbons

Daffodils, narcissi, jonquils, tulips and primroses all lend themselves nicely to decorations for a yellow and white table in the springtime of the year. A pretty white bowl filled with yellow narcissi or tulips makes a pretty centerpiece as also do daffodils. A pretty effect is also obtained by using a pretty white basket and filling it with yellow blossoms, or a yellow basket may be filled with white spring blossoms. If candles are used they may be

white with yellow holders and white shades.
Plain gilt-edged cards with the stem of a yellow blossom passed through a slit in one corner
make nice place-cards. The guests' names
may be written on in gilt ink. Have at each
plate tiny white baskets filled with yellow bonbons, or yellow baskets filled with white bonbons. If preferred white boxes decorated with
flights of yellow butterflies or with yellow blossoms may be used. If possible use gilt-edged
china or china with a very narrow line of gilt
on it.

In making the cream sauce for the potato
croquettes if not yellow enough add a little
yellow vegetable coloring.

GRAPEFRUIT CUP

Grapefruit   White grapes
4 tablespoonfuls pineapple juice

Cut nice grapefruits in halves crossways, remove the seeds and with a sharp knife separate
the pulp from the skin. Remove, separate
carefully into sections and free from the mem-

brane. Keep the fruit in good-sized pieces.
Take an equal quantity of white grapes, skin
and remove seeds, and add to the grapefruit,
then add the pineapple juice. The amount of
grape juice given ought to be enough for six
grapefruits. Fill this mixture into grapefruit
cups and top with white grapes.

Daisy Canapes

6 eggs	Mayonnaise
Bread	1 dozen sardines
1 teaspoonful lemon-juice	Salt and cayenne

Cut thin slices of bread into daisy shape
with a sharp knife or a daisy cutter. If a
knife is used outline the daisy on a cardboard
pattern. Fry a delicate brown on both sides
in hot butter. Cut the hard-boiled eggs into
halves, and chop the whites very fine, and run
the yolks through a sieve. Remove the bones
and skins from the sardines and run into a
paste with a little mayonnaise, season with the
lemon-juice, salt and a pinch of cayenne.
Spread the bread with this, then place the
whites of the eggs on the petals, and the yolks

in the center. This is an appetizer as well as pretty.

ORANGE ROLLOVERS

Rich pie pastry	Candied orange peel
English walnuts	Sugar
1 teaspoonful orange-juice	1 teaspoonful pineapple-juice

To a half cupful of candied orange peel add a few chopped walnut meats, about a fourth of a cupful, then add the fruit juices and a little powdered sugar. Both the orange and nuts should be chopped very fine. Roll out some rich pie pastry and cut into squares. Spread some of the orange and nut mixture over each square, and roll up like a jelly roll. Bake in a moderate oven until a delicate brown. Nice to serve with a salad course.

SPRING DELIGHT

1 tablespoonful gelatin	6 eggs
2 cupfuls of boiling water	2/3 cupful of sugar
1 teaspoonful vanilla extract	1 teaspoonful lemon extract
	Yellow coloring
½ cupful of nut-meats	

Soak the gelatin in a little cold water; when dissolved add the boiling water and the sugar.

Place over the fire and bring to the boil, then fold in the stiffly beaten whites of the eggs. Beat up until it begins to stiffen, then divide into two portions; color one portion yellow with yellow vegetable coloring and flavor with lemon; leave the other portion white and flavor with vanilla. Pour in alternate layers into a square mold, sprinkling a few chopped nuts between each layer. A little candied orange or lemon peel will also add to it. Set on ice until firm, then turn out of mold, cut into form of bricks. Place on plates and heap around them whipped cream.

PINK AND WHITE

Tomato Bouillon   Wafers
Creamed Fish with Pink Sauce
Pimiento Sandwiches   Strawberry Sandwiches
Cottage Cheese Salad
Strawberry Gelatin Pudding   Peach Blossom Cakes
Pink and White Bonbons

Nothing can make more delightful table decorations for a pink and white color scheme than sweet peas. Just a big bunch of pink and white blossoms arranged loosely in a wide-mouthed bowl, or a dainty basket filled with the dainty, fragrant blossoms will make a charming centerpiece. If you wish something more elaborate suspend over the table a wreath of sweet peas, and from this have sweet pea ropes to extend from the wreath to each plate where they may be attached to little baskets filled with sweet peas in water colors, or a blossom or two passed through a slit in one corner.

If one does not care to use flowers altogether, a very pretty scheme may be carried out with pink ribbon and paper. A large pink rose Jack Horner pie may be used for the centerpiece, with narrow pink and white ribbons leading to each plate, where they can be tied to the handles of little baskets in delicate shades of pink, holding white bonbons.

COTTAGE CHEESE SALAD

Cottage cheese	Pimientoes
Celery	White boiled dressing

Pass the pimientoes through a food chopper, and mix into the cottage cheese until it is a pale pink in color, add a little good boiled dressing and chopped celery. Place on white lettuce leaves.

STRAWBERRY GELATIN PUDDING

1 cupful mashed straw- berries	1 cupful sugar
1 lemon	1 cupful cream
1 tablespoonful gelatin	¼ cupful water

Soak the gelatin in the cold water. Place in a double boiler one cupful water, the sugar and the juice, and bring to boil, then stir in the gelatin, strain and add to the strawberry pulp. Chill and when it begins to stiffen up fold in the whipped cream. Pour into mold and turn out, and surround with whipped cream.

STRAWBERRY SANDWICHES

These are made by spreading thin slices of buttered bread with strawberry preserves mixed with a few chopped almond meats, although these may be omitted if liked.

RED AND GREEN

Lettuce and Pimiento Sandwiches   Creamed Beets
Lobster in Pâté Shells
Tomato Salad   Currant Wafers
Olives   Radishes
Strawberries   Cake Confectionery

For a red and green color scheme red tulips, red roses, geraniums or any red flowers will be appropriate. The flowers will look pretty arranged in a deep bowl or basket. Use the tulips in colors ranging from the bright scarlet to the very dark red. Use pale green candles in red holders. Serve the strawberries in dark green baskets or pails. Touch the edges of the place-cards with red or green, and if liked, the names may be written on them with red ink.

TOMATO SALAD

Medium-sized tomatoes   Lettuce
Green peppers   Cucumbers
Celery   Green mayonnaise

Choose nice ripe, but firm tomatoes. Dip quickly into boiling water and remove the skins. Scoop out the insides and sprinkle with salt and pepper. Chop together an equal quantity of cucumbers, celery and green peppers from which the seeds have been removed. Mix into this enough green mayonnaise to make of the right consistency and fill in the cavities in the tomatoes. Chill and serve on lettuce leaves on individual plates.

WHITE MENU TO BE USED WITH A BLUE AND WHITE SCHEME

Clam Bouillon in Blue Cups

Small Biscuits   Pineapple Preserves

White Chicken Salad

Creamed Potatoes in Blue Ramekins

White Ice-Cream   Angel Food Cake

Sea Foam Candy in Blue Boxes

Since the tulip comes from Holland it is a good idea to use a vase or bowl of white tulips and introduce a " Dutch " scheme with them. Use blue and white china and have at each plate a little blue and white windmill. Serve the ices in tulip cases and use white bonbon boxes decorated with tiny Dutch figures in blue. The name cards may be decorated with little Dutch scenes, or Holland post-cards may be used with the guests' names written on them. The centerpiece may be a little wooden shoe filled with tulips instead of the blue bowl or vase, if preferred. If candles are used, have both candles and shades in white, but have the shades decorated with little, quaint Dutch figures or blue windmills cut out of dark blue paper.

A Japanese Luncheon

Menu

Iced Cantaloup

Jambalaya of Fowls and Rice   Sardine Sandwiches

Okonomara Salad

O'cha Ice-Cream   Sembei

Crystallized Fruits

Tea

One can obtain so many pretty and artistic things with which to decorate a table for a Japanese luncheon that one scarcely knows which to choose. If you wish to use flowers on the table, use cherry blossoms, wisteria, chrysanthemums, irises, Japanese lilies, or any of the favorite blossoms of Japan. From the chandelier may be suspended Japanese fern balls.

For this luncheon use Japanese ware if possible, with its quaint, queer designs of flowers, dragons and figures. One can pick up at Japanese stores many unique little vases, cups and such like that would add to the table decorations.

The place-cards should be decorated with the quaint Japanese figures, and the favors may be tiny Japanese fans and may serve as place-cards as well as favors if liked.

Since cherry blossoms are so closely associated with the Japanese, being to them what roses are to the Westerner, it is nice to have cherry-blossom decorations in connection with a Japanese luncheon. Select as perfect a shaped branch of cherry blossoms as you can obtain and plant in pretty pot. Place in the center of the table, decorating it with Japanese figures. Under this miniature cherry-tree place a number of Japanese dolls dressed in their native costumes. Have at each plate a tiny Japanese vase holding a spray of blossoms. Tiny fans decorated with cherry blossoms may be used for place-cards or favors.

The chrysanthemum and things Japanese go very appropriately together in table decorations. A very pretty and novel decoration is obtained by placing in the center of the table a pretty and odd-shaped lantern, partly filling it with sand or something to keep it firm, then place in it chrysanthemums in colors that harmonize with the color of the lantern and the other decorations. At each plate have an odd-shaped Japanese vase filled with one or two perfect chrysanthemums, or tiny Japanese parasols may be inverted and filled with blossoms. On one corner of the place-cards paste little Japanese figures and in the other corner slip through the stem of a chrysanthemum. If candles are used have the candle shades decorated with chrysanthemums or Japanese figures.

O'CHA ICE-CREAM

1 quart cream   1 pint Oolong tea
¼ cupful ginger sirup   6 eggs

Scald the cream in a double boiler, add to it the tea which should be quite strong, then stir in the ginger sirup and the six eggs, well-beaten; cook in the double boiler until the custard coats a spoon. Sweeten to taste, and cool; pour into ice-cream freezer and freeze as you would any other ice-cream. Serve in glasses with bits of preserved ginger on top.

SEMBEI

1 pint rice flour   4 eggs
1 pint milk   ¼ cupful sugar
½ teaspoonful nutmeg

If you cannot obtain the rice flour, run rice through a coffee grinder or meat chopper. Beat the eggs up well, and add the sugar, nutmeg and the milk; add the flour which should make a dough that will roll out quite thin. Cut in fancy shapes and bake a delicate brown.

JAMBALAYA OF FOWL AND RICE

½ cupful rice
2 tablespoonfuls butter
½ cupful English walnut-
    meats

1 pint cooked chicken
1 tablespoonful minced
    onion
Salt and pepper

Wash the rice thoroughly and place in a sufficient amount of boiling water to preserve the shape of the kernels when melted. Salt well and drain, pour the melted butter over the rice. Season with pepper and the onion. Mix the chicken and nut-meats broken into bits. Put the rice in a deep dish, then cover with the meat mixture. Cover and place in the oven for about twenty minutes.

OKONOMARA SALAD

Madarin oranges
Preserved ginger
Lemon sirup

Litchi nuts
Cucumbers

Remove the skin from the oranges and slice. Remove seeds and membrane. Cook the nut-meats in lemon sirup for ten minutes. If you cannot obtain the litchi nuts use other nut-meats. Cut the cucumbers into cubes, and add to the orange and nut-meats, using an equal quantity of each. Add half the quantity of preserved ginger; that is, if you use a cupful each of the other ingredients use only one-half cupful of preserved ginger.

A Snowball Luncheon

Snowball Hoppy

Snowball Croquettes   Snowball Biscuit

Snowball Salad

Snowball Ice-Cream   Snowball Cake

Popcorn Balls

There is nothing more suggestive of coolness than a snowball luncheon. If this luncheon is to be given on the porch decorate it profusely with snowballs made out of frosted crepe paper or with cotton batting sprinkled with isinglass to represent frost or snow. With the snowballs use cool green, which may be found in the ferns and vines.

Use paper snowballs for the center of the table unless the luncheon is given in snowball season, then use the real flowers. Green ferns tucked in and out among the blossoms will add to the cool effect. Have at each plate a popcorn ball rolled in sugar; these should be placed on a mat of green.

The menu carried out in snowballs will add to decorations of the table.

SNOWBALL HOPPY

1 pint pineapple-juice	1 cupful lemon-juice
1 pint orange-juice	1 cupful sugar
Shaved ice	Fresh fruits

Place the sugar in a kettle with one-half cupful water and boil to a thick sirup; then add the other juices, and cool. Form snowballs of finely shaved ice, and place one in tall glasses, and then fill two-thirds full of the juice. Add bits of fresh fruit or whole strawberries or cherries. Serve at the beginning of the luncheon as you would a fruit soup.

SNOWBALL CROQUETTES

1 pint mashed potatoes	1 cupful white sauce
Powdered sugar	Egg-whites

Season the mashed potatoes and mix the white sauce into them. Form in shape of snowballs, roll in bread-crumbs and egg-whites. Fry in deep fat, and while hot roll in powdered sugar until completely covered. Rice may be used instead of potatoes.

SNOWBALL SALAD

Cottage cheese	White mayonnaise
Lettuce leaves	Salt and white pepper

Season the cottage cheese with salt and pepper and add white mayonnaise or boiled dressing. Form into shape of balls. Serve on lettuce leaves.

Use the " ball " scoop which caterers use to form the ice-cream snowballs. The snowball cakes may be cut from white angel food cake, iced in white, and rolled in cocoanut.

A FERN LUNCHEON

Chicken Bouillon with Bits of Parsley on Top

Creamed Peas   Fried Chicken

Cucumber Salad

Ice-Cream   White Cake

Green Mints

Around the edge of the porch suspend fern

balls and hanging baskets filled with ferns and trailing vines. In one corner of the porch have a fern-covered rockery and spring, which can be made by building up a mound of stones and sticking the crevices full of ferns. In one side of the mound a hole can be left in which is placed a wide-mouthed crock cleverly concealed with ferns. This crock is filled with lemonade, kept cool in a bed of ice. By the side of this artificial spring hangs a gourd dipper, from which the guests can help themselves.

In the center of the table have a box made of birch-bark and filled with maiden-hair ferns; sprays of maiden-hair and asparagus ferns can be scattered here and there over the white cloth and at each end of the table stand a vase or receptacle made of birch-bark filled with ferns.

PAPER, PORCH AND LAWN PARTIES

There are great possibilities in the way of paper parties for the summer months since such light, airy effects can be so readily procured with paper decorations, as well as quite artistic table effects, and there is an inexpensiveness about them that has nothing of cheapness in it. They are quite the thing for those who are compelled to do their entertaining in a cottage by lake or sea where china and silver are not very plentiful with the hostess, and also quite convenient for the hostess that keeps no servants, since there are very few dishes to wash up after the affair, as nearly everything can be served in pretty paper cases.

The invitations to such a party can be sent out in tiny Japanese paper lanterns. Decorate the porch and lawn with paper flags and pennants, paper bells and Japanese paper lanterns, and a profusion of paper flowers can be used. A pretty bower can be made by covering it with crepe paper and then garlanding it with paper flowers. Butterflies made out of crepe paper and touched up with water colors to make them more brilliant and life-like can be suspended from the ceiling of the porch by means of strong, black thread and will look quite charming as they flutter in the breeze. Japanese paper screens are also appropriate and add to the charm of the affair. Present each guest as he or she arrives with a paper fan; partners can be matched if liked by quotations of a "Summery" nature written on these.

Floral tables are appropriate for almost any entertainment, and they give an opportunity for a choice of the usually accepted color schemes. If several small tables are used, a different flower or color scheme can be used on each table. Plain white crepe paper will make the nicest table cover or background. A table covered with pure white paper, with a paper decorated with the flowers to be used on the table draped around it will make a pretty effect, or the decorated paper ribbon that one can get in crepe paper now can be crossed in the center of the table. A water-lily scheme is especially appropriate for a summer gathering. Decorate the center of the table with a bouquet of water lilies, and serve the ices in cases made to represent water lilies, the yellow ice-cream forming their golden hearts. Pink and white lilies can both be used. Roses are charming for flower cases, and cherry sherbet served in American beauty cases will be lovely, or lemon sherbet served in yellow roses. Plain cases wreathed with sweet peas, forget-me-nots, pansies or small rosebuds are especially pleasing.

Effective Table Decorations for Autumn Tables

The decorations of the autumn tables should suggest largely the overflowing bounty as we find it symbolized in nature at this season of the year, and the color schemes as found in the yellow and golds of the ripening grains, golden-rod, pumpkins and the autumn leaves; in the purple and white of the grapes; in the red of the apples and the bright autumn berries, and such like. This is one of the seasons of the year when the hostess can have pretty table effects with very little outlay of money and very little trouble.

The chrysanthemum is certainly the queen of fall flowers, with its little buttons, its larger blooms, its great balls of yellow and red, of the mingled colors, of pale straw, of royal purple and its plumes of snow. It certainly deserves a place of honor on the autumn tables. A great bowl of these flowers, ranging in color from cream through all the rich dull shades of yellow to a reddish copper color will make a fine centerpiece for the autumn tables. The regular chrysanthemum ice cups are very nice indeed, and are easy to make. The entrées, salads and ices may be served in these, using different colors. Candle shades may be made in the form of the " ragged " variety.

RED AND BROWN TABLE SCHEME

Apple Appetizer
Brown Bread Sandwiches with Pimiento Filling
Baked Beans Garnished with Beet Pickles
Ham Soufflé   Tomato Salad
Date Fluff   Chocolate Nut Cake
Red Peppermints in Brown Receptacles

Brown and red makes a charming color for

an autumn table, and is not so common as
the others. Arrange in the center of the table
a mat of red maple or sumach leaves, and on
this place an odd-shaped raffia basket filled
with shining red apples. Have at one end of
the table a red bowl or basket edged with
bittersweet vines and berries, filled with chocolate candies. At the other end of the table
have a similar bowl or basket filled with
nuts.

String cranberries and peanuts alternately
and entwine around principal dishes or bring
down from the chandelier to each plate and at-
tach to pine cones. Use long pine cones for
candlesticks, mounting them on red cardboard
maple leaves for standards. Use red candles,
and place the candles on mats of brown
autumn leaves. Brown or red autumn leaves
may be used for place-cards, lettering the
names on with black or white ink. If preferred the scheme may be carried out with red
chrysanthemums instead of fruit. Place the
chrysanthemums in a receptacle made of birch-
bark or raffia, or any brown bowl or basket

will be suitable. Have at each plate a little vase made out of a cocoanut shell, filled with a few of the red chrysanthemums, or red peppermints. Unique candle holders may be made out of chestnut burrs, soaked in water until they become pliable, then insert the candle and press together until it is held firmly in place. Tie together until it is dry. If they refuse to stand level, glue to pasteboard foundations. Red candles look pretty in these holders.

A brown and red scheme can be developed nicely with nuts. Arrange in the center of table a mat of red maple or sumach leaves, and on this place a pretty basket or bowl filled with mixed nuts. Have at each plate a small fancy basket in dull red filled with chocolate bonbons and nut candies.

Little squares or oblong cards of birch-bark decorated with acorns glued on make nice place-cards. Pretty baskets may be made by glueing acorns over a pasteboard foundation. It will not be a bit difficult to plan up a nut menu for this luncheon. Nut sandwiches, nut salads, nut croquettes, nut cakes and nut ice-cream may all be used if liked.

APPLE APPETIZER

Tart apple jelly   Currant jelly
Red apples   Chopped almonds

Take as many nice red apples as there are people to be served, cut a slice off the stem end and scoop out as much of the flesh as possible. Mix together equal quantities of tart apple jelly, currant jelly or lemon jelly, and mix with half the quantity of chopped almonds. Fill this into the apple shells. Place on a brown maple leaf and serve one to each person as a relish for the meal.

HAM SOUFFLÉ

1 tablespoonful butter   1 tablespoonful flour
1 cupful milk   1 cupful cooked ham
1 tablespoonful chopped   ½ cupful bread-crumbs
  parsley   Salt and pepper
3 eggs

Make a cream sauce with the butter, flour

and milk, season with the salt, pepper and parsley. Add the bread-crumbs and the ham, chopped fine. Add the yolks of two eggs, beaten, then the stiffly whipped whites. Pour into a greased bake-dish and bake in the oven for about twenty minutes. A tablespoonful of soup stock will add to the flavor of the soufflé.

DATE FLUFF

1 cupful stoned dates	1 cupful sugar
5 eggs	1 teaspoonful cream of tartar
1 teaspoonful vanilla	Chopped nut-meats

Stew the dates until tender, then pass through a sieve and add the sugar and cream of tartar (a tablespoonful of lemon-juice can be used instead of the cream of tartar). Stir in the yolks of two eggs, then the stiffly beaten whites, and whip up until light. Place in a ramekin or bake-dish and sprinkle the top over with chopped nuts, and bake in the oven fifteen or twenty minutes. Serve with whipped cream or a sauce.

Brown Bread Canapes

Boston brown bread	Whipped cream
Made mustard	Grated ham
Nut-meats	Salt

Take as many slices of Boston brown bread as will serve the guests invited. Whip up some rich cream until stiff, and mix with it enough made mustard to make a rich yellow. Spread this thick upon the brown bread and then sprinkle over with the grated ham. Place the half of a walnut meat in the center of each canape.

Chestnut Croquettes

2 cupfuls boiled chestnut-pulp	3 tablespoonfuls grated cream cheese
Pimientoes	2 eggs
Thick cream sauce	Salt

After passing the boiled chestnuts through a sieve, add the cheese, the beaten yolks of the eggs and enough cream sauce to mold nicely. Season with salt. When molding place a bit of pimiento in the center of each croquette. Roll in egg and then in bread-crumbs and fry in deep fat a delicate brown. Serve with or without sauce.

YELLOW AND GREEN TABLE SCHEME

Cream Consommé

Creamed Peas in Carrot Cups

Egg and Lettuce Sandwiches

Creamed Chicken in Green Pepper Cases

Yellow Tomato Preserves   Sweet Pickled Carrots

Olives

Pumpkin Custard   Lemon Pie

Cake Decorated with Candy Carrots

Yellow Bonbons

It is wonderful the color schemes that may be carried out with vegetables. A pretty yellow and green scheme may be carried out with pumpkins, carrots and little yellow tomatoes, with plenty of cress or parsley to give the necessary touch of green. Place a large pumpkin in the center of the table and around this arrange a mound of parsley or cress. Almost

concealed by the parsley or cress have a row
of the small yellow tomatoes or carrots. At
each plate have a small pumpkin vase filled
with sprays of fern or parsley. The place-
cards may be pale yellow with a spray of
parsley inserted through a slit in one corner.
Serve the yellow bonbons in little green baskets or boxes. Orange or grapefruit baskets
lined with waxed paper make nice holders for
the bonbons or for the ice.

Grape Luncheon

Grape Menu

Sardine Sandwiches   Stuffed Eggplant
                    Spiced Fruits
Grape Salad   Biscuits with Grape Jelly
      Grape Sherbet   Grape Jelly Roll
                    Glacé Grapes

Very pretty purple and white table schemes
can be carried out with purple and white
grapes. Place in the center of the table a circular mirror and conceal the edges with bunches

of purple grapes or purple and white grapes
alternately, with grape leaves interspersed
among them. Suspend a cluster of as perfect
clusters of purple and white grapes as you can
obtain from the chandelier, using purple and
lavender ribbon for that purpose. This cluster
should be right over the mirror and its reflec-
tion in it should give a pretty effect. Have at
each plate a bunch of crystallized grapes with
a tiny bow of purple ribbon tied to the stems.
It would be nice to have the purple and white
grapes to alternate around the table. Have
the place-cards to represent grape leaves. Use
white and purple grapes in making the salad.

A low green and white basket placed on a
mat of autumn leaves or ferns and filled with
red, purple and white makes a simple but delightful centerpiece. When this kind of a centerpiece is used a bunch of grapes can be
placed on a large maple leaf at each plate or
small green and white baskets may be filled
with crystallized grapes. These should be
placed on mats to correspond with the centerpiece.

Maple Leaf Luncheon

Orange Cups

Browned Chops   Rice Croquettes

Baked Bean Salad   Stuffed Tomatoes

Rolls

Chocolate Ice-Cream in Shape of Maple Leaves

Sponge Cake Leaves   Maple Bonbons

Salted Almonds

A charming effect may be produced with maple leaves in the following manner: select a branch from a maple tree that is as tree-like as possible and insert in a standard of wood or in a pot of sand; cover this with green crepe paper and then with vines so that the standard or pot will be entirely concealed. Place this miniature tree in the center of the table and scatter brilliant maple leaves here and there over the cloth. Have under the tree two or three tiny gilded wheelbarrows filled with gay maple leaves; have little gilded forks leaning against these. At each corner of the table have toy wheelbarrows filled with fruits.

The place-cards should be in form of maple leaves, colored in warm browns and brilliant scarlets. The candle shades should be decorated with maple leaves. Pretty little "bushel" baskets may be filled with nuts and bonbons and placed at each plate. The place-cards may be decorated with maple leaves, or be in form of maple leaves as desired.

POPCORN LUNCHEON

Menu

Cream Bouillon with Popcorn
Popcorn Canapes   Popcorn Marguerites
Salad with Buttered Popcorn
Popcorn Ice-Cream Balls   Popcorn Cake
Popcorn Dainty

A delightful and unique luncheon may be carried out entirely with popcorn both in decorations and menu. The popcorn intended for the decorations should be popped several days ahead of time and kept in a damp place so that the grains will be tough enough to string nicely without breaking. These strings of popcorn should be touched up with gilt and colored paints, and then festooned about the dining-room and also about the chandelier. From the chandelier bring a string down to each plate to the ends of which can be attached popcorn balls that contain the favors. Some of the popcorn can be strung alternately with red berries, and used with the other with good effect.

The centerpiece for the table may be a mound of popcorn balls arranged on a mat of red maple leaves—ferns could be used instead, or a wreath of bittersweet vine and berries could be used with good effect around the base of the mound. Some of the popcorn balls can be rolled in rock candy while still sticky, and will then resemble balls of ice, others can be rolled in cocoanut, and a few in colored sugar to give a touch of red. At each plate have a little popcorn basket filled with red and white crystallized popcorn; these little baskets can be formed out of nougat, molded while still warm, and the white popcorn stuck on the outside before the nougat has hardened. Wire should be used for the handles, around which twine narrow red ribbon. Finish with a tiny bow at the top. These popcorn baskets will give quite a decorative effect to the table. The favors may be concealed inside of popcorn balls at each place. The favors should be first wrapped in paraffine paper, and the sugared popcorn pressed around them until the ball is formed; these balls should then be rolled in red sugar while still sticky. Letter the names on the place-cards with the grains of red, un-popped corn glued on—the smallest grains obtainable being used for the purpose. The edges of the cards may be touched up with gilt paint.

The cream bouillon should be served with perfect grains of freshly popped corn floating on the top. Freshly buttered popcorn should be served with the salad, which can be made of nuts. The ice-cream can be served in shape of balls and covered with freshly popped corn giving them an excellent resemblance to pop-corn balls. A little red sugar can be sprinkled over these balls to make them look like the others. Cake with a popcorn icing may be served, or popcorn and nuts mixed. Recipes are given for the other dishes mentioned in menu.

Popcorn Canapes

1 cupful good milk
3 boned sardines
1 tablespoonful tomato
  catsup
½ teaspoonful Worcester-
  shire sauce

1 teaspoonful salt
1 tablespoonful flour
1 tablespoonful butter
A pinch of red pepper
1 tablespoonful cheese
Fresh popcorn

Make a cream sauce with the butter, flour and milk. Stir until smooth and thick, then season; to this add the boned sardines, and enough freshly popped corn to make a good paste to spread. Cut hot buttered toast into squares and circles and spread with this paste.

Popcorn Marguerites

1 cupful of sugar
¼ teaspoonful cream of
  tartar
1 cupful popcorn
½ cupful nut-meats

½ cupful water
1 egg
1 teaspoonful vanilla
Pinch of salt

Boil the sugar, water and cream of tartar to the firm ball stage. Pour over the beaten white of the egg; then when it begins to stiffen up, add the popcorn and nut-meats which should be passed through a food-chopper, and the vanilla.   Spread on saltines or any wafers or crackers.

Popcorn Dainty

2 cupfuls maple sugar	1 cupful cream
¼ teaspoonful cream of tartar	2 cupfuls popcorn

Cook all but the popcorn to the hard ball stage.   Remove from fire and beat up until it begins to turn creamy, then stir in the large crisp kernels of popcorn.   Turn into a square or oblong pan, well-buttered; then press until flat on top, but not hard enough to crush the kernels.   Cut into bars with sharp knife.

Table Decorations for Corn Luncheons

In giving a corn luncheon both the husks and corn itself can be used very effectively in decorations.   The creamy inside husks can be woven in such a way as to make pretty mats, baskets, cases for salads and ices and lamp or candle shades.   In making the baskets pasteboard foundations should be used or what would be better still use light baskets for the foundation and you will have a true basket shape. Cheap baskets can be used for the foundation. A woven husk basket filled with golden-rod or yellow chrysanthemums, wreathed around the edge and handle with smilax or any delicate vine, will make a fine centerpiece for the table. Tiny baskets made of the braided corn-husks should serve as receptacles for the bonbons. At each cover can be a doily or mat of woven corn-husks; these can be decorated with water colors if desired —a bit of waving corn would be nice or a spray of golden-rod. Little cases for the salads and ices can be made by sewing the braided strands of corn-husks on plain paper cases which can be easily procured from any shop that makes a specialty of such things or can be easily made at home with a little cardboard. These can be decorated to suit the fancy; the edges are pretty touched up with irregular bands of orange, green or gold. The candle or lamp shades should be decorated to match or at least harmonize with the decorations on the doilies and cases. The name cards can be cut from the corn-husks with the names lettered

on in gold and green. Little booklets with
corn-husk covers, tied with green ribbon, will
make delightful favors. This booklet should
contain as many blank pages as there are
guests and should have a small pencil attached so that it can be passed around for the
favorite corn recipe of each guest, the hostess
having hers already written on the first page
and signed with her name.

Another very pleasing and novel red and yellow color effect can be carried out with corn
for a luncheon. Soak red corn for a week, or
until soft enough to string on wire. The wire
should be very fine. Form these strings of
corn into a basket shape; a foundation can be
used to shape over if desired. Fill this basket
with yellow apples, pears, bananas and oranges, or the basket can be made of yellow
corn and red fruits used or with red chrysanthemums. A string of red corn can be entwined in and out among the central dishes;
ears of red and yellow popcorn should be suspended from the chandelier over the table.
Unique place-cards may be made by mounting

red popcorn on yellow cards to form the name, using mucilage to fasten the names on the cards.

MENUS FOR CORN LUNCHEONS

Menu No. 1

Cream of Corn Soup

Corn Oysters   Sliced Corned Beef

Corn in Tomato Cups

Corn Puffs

Corn-starch Dainty Dessert   Corn-starch Cake

Crystallized Popcorn

Menu No. 2

Corn and Tomato Soup   Wafers

Corn Fritters

Baked Corn with Chicken   Corn Salad

Cornmeal Muffins   Quince Honey

Steamed Indian Corn Pudding

Little Cakes

Fruit

Menu No. 3

Corn Popovers   Grape Jelly

Hominy Croquettes

Nut and Celery Salad (in corn-husk cases)

Buttered Popcorn

Peach Ice-Cream (in corn-husk cases)

Corn-starch Layer Cake

Bonbons   Salted Nuts

CORN OYSTERS

1 cupful corn	1 teaspoonful salt
2 cupfuls flour	1 cupful milk
2 teaspoonfuls baking-powder	2 eggs
	¼ teaspoonful pepper

Use either canned corn or fresh corn from the ear, add the milk, the well-beaten eggs; then stir in the dry ingredients well mixed together. Drop by spoonfuls into deep fat and fry a golden brown. Drain on brown paper and serve hot.

CORN IN TOMATO CUPS

1 cupful of corn	1 cupful bread-crumbs
1 tablespoonful butter	½ teaspoonful salt
⅛ teaspoonful pepper	1 teaspoonful grated onion

Take as many medium-sized tomatoes as there are people to be served and remove the seeds, after taking a thin slice off the stem-end. Mix the corn and other ingredients well together. Fill into the tomato cups and bake in a moderate oven.

CORN-STARCH DESSERT

4 tablespoonfuls corn-
  starch
1 cupful sugar
2 lemons

1 pint boiling water
3 eggs
Pinch of salt

Mix the corn-starch in cold water and when dissolved stir into the boiling water to which has been added the sugar and salt and the grated rind of one lemon and the juice. Boil a few minutes, stirring constantly; then pour over the stiffly beaten whites of the eggs. Mix thoroughly and pour into a mold. Serve with a sauce or whipped cream. If you wish it a cream color add the yolk of one of the eggs.

CORN FRITTERS

2 cupfuls cooked corn
1 teaspoonful salt
2 teaspoonfuls baking-
  powder

1 cupful milk
3 eggs
2 cupfuls flour

To the corn-pulp add the milk, yolks of the eggs, salt, and then stir in the flour in which the baking-powder has been sifted. Mix thoroughly, then fold in the egg-whites. Drop by spoonfuls into very hot fat and drain. Serve with maple sugar or sirup.

BAKED CORN WITH CHICKEN

3 tablespoonfuls flour	Cheese
3 tablespoonfuls butter	1 cupful corn
1 cupful cooked white of chicken	1½ cupfuls milk
	Salt and pepper
Bread-crumbs	

Make a sauce with the flour, butter and milk, stir until smooth and thick, season well with salt and pepper. Take two-thirds of this sauce and mix into the corn, add the chicken chopped fine. Put in a buttered bake-dish, cover with the remaining sauce and some grated cheese and cover with buttered bread-crumbs. Bake in the oven until a delicate brown.

CORN SALAD

2 cupfuls cooked corn	½ cupful of celery
½ teaspoonful salt	¼ teaspoonful paprika
1 tablespoonful gelatin	1 cupful boiling water
Mayonnaise dressing	Tomato

Dissolve the gelatin in two tablespoonfuls of cold water, stir into the boiling water, add the corn and celery when it begins to stiffen up. Pour into individual molds. Chill and turn out each mold onto a slice of tomato marinated with French dressing. Place on lettuce leaves and heap mayonnaise around each mold.

BIRTHDAY FLOWER LUNCHEONS

Menu for Pansy Luncheon

Grapefruit Cup

Chicken Croquettes with Brown Sauce   Celery

Baked Beans in Brown or Yellow Ramekins

Brown Bread Nut Sandwiches   Cream Cheese Balls

Banana Salad with Peanut Mayonnaise

Chocolate Ice-Cream   Sunshine Cake

Chocolate Bonbons

Candied Orange and Lemon Peel

Cocoa with Whipped Cream

Nothing can be more appropriate than floral birthday tables and they are nice for both old and young. A very effective color scheme can be carried out in yellow and brown by using yellow pansies. Ice the birthday cake with chocolate icing and wreathe the cake with yellow pansies—a few blossoms scattered over the cake will add to the effect. Yellow candles may be used on the cake. Use place-cards in brown, with the edges touched up in gilt, with the names lettered on in gold ink, and they also may be decorated with yellow pansies. Use the pretty glazed brown ware with the edges touched up with gilt for the entrées. Have at each plate a little brown bowl or basket filled with candied orange and lemon peel, preserved ginger and chocolate candies.

MENU FOR RED RAMBLER ROSE LUNCHEON

Pimiento Canapes

Lobster in Shells　　　　　　　Tomato Pineapple Salad

Creamed Corn in Red Pepper Cases

Beet Pickles

Strawberry Sherbet　　　　　　　　　Pound Cake

Candied Cherries

A very effective birthday table scheme may be carried out with rambler roses. Have the birthday cake iced in white and placed on a mat of ferns, then wreathe with red roses. Either red or white candles can be used on the cake or they can be alternated. At each plate can be a dull red basket filled with candied cherries. Use white place-cards with a single rose thrust through a slit in the corner. Serve the strawberry sherbet in red rose cases and decorate the birthday cake with candied cherries. If artificial light is used it would be nice to have red candles with white shades.

TRIMMINGS FOR BIRTHDAY CAKES

Trimmings add greatly to birthday cakes and many novel effects may be obtained without a great deal of trouble.

Birthday candles that may be eaten, holders and all, will surprise and please the children. Make the candles of marzipan paste and use round marshmallows for the holders, sticking the candles in little holes in the center. Almond-meats may serve as the wicks of the candles. If the candles do not seem firm place a little icing around the hole. Follow any favorite cake recipe, and ice the cake in pink and white and decorate with as many of these little candles as the age of the boy or girl requires. These candles may be lighted if liked, for the oil in the almond nuts will usually cause them to burn for a short time, but whether they are lighted or not they make a pretty decoration.

Here is an idea for a girl's birthday cake. Bake a round cake and put on a thick icing. Place tiny china dolls, one doll for each guest, all around the edge of the cake, facing outward. These little dolls should be dressed in crepe paper costumes and little cones made of paraffine paper slipped in under the skirts will aid as supports. If the dolls are small and the frosting thick they may not need any support. When a birthday cake is decorated on the top, the birthday candles may encircle the cake instead of being placed on top.

Birthday flowers may be formed on birthday cakes with small candy mites, or the flat oval candies, which are obtainable in any confectionery store, in different colors. Angelica may be used for the leaves. Names and dates may also be lettered on with these candies.

One can obtain little silver and gold candies that are nice for this purpose.

A cake decorated with round flat mints with little clown faces outlined on them in chocolate or fruit coloring will delight the children. Ice the cake before putting on the mints and press them in while it is soft.

One may form all sorts of animals out of marshmallows with which to decorate the cake. Place the marshmallows on a pan and let stand in a slow oven until they soften up; then form into bunnies, bears, rats, mice or chicks. One can use allspice for eyes and the ears and tails may be cut out of candied fruits. Roses may be formed out of marshmallows also, and can be dipped into colored fondants and used on the cake, making the leaves out of angelica, citron or candied mint-leaves.

IV

CATERING FOR WEDDINGS AND
OTHER BRIDAL AFFAIRS

CHAPTER IV

CATERING FOR WEDDINGS AND OTHER BRIDAL AFFAIRS

DECORATIONS FOR WEDDING TABLES

WHITE and green is always a popular color scheme for bridal tables. This can be carried out nicely with white roses, valley lilies, white sweet peas, white carnations, white irises, asters, chrysanthemums, gladioli and other white flowers in their season. Pretty effects may also be obtained with elder blossoms, dogwood blossoms and white clover. Use with the white blossoms vines and ferns for the necessary touch of green.

For the gold and white effects can be used daisies, yellow roses, golden poppies, buttercups, daffodils, yellow tulips, jonquils, chrysanthemums, asters, golden-rod, marigolds and yellow irises; these can be used with white blossoms, or the white part of the scheme may be obtained with the linen, china and the food.

To obtain the gold and green effect use ferns and vines with the yellow blossoms, and for gold and red effects use in connection with the yellow blossoms red roses, geraniums, carnations, poinsettias, tulips, dahlias, gladioli, or any red blossoms in season.

Pink and white color schemes are always very popular for wedding affairs. For carrying out this scheme can be used pink roses, pink sweet peas, apple, peach and cherry blossoms, trailing arbutus, gladioli, pink lilies, carnations, azaleas, spirea and pink begonias.

Purple and white effects may be produced with violets, lilacs, wisteria, purple irises, hyacinths, asters, pansies, or any other purple blossoms.

There are many effective ways in which the flowers may be arranged. A very pretty effect may be obtained by suspending a fancy basket from the light fixtures over the table. Hang it so it will be only a few inches above the table and have the vines to trail down upon the cloth. Any kind of blossoms desired may be used in the basket. The possibilities of this hanging decoration are numerous and charming; for instance, in the autumn the basket could be filled with autumn flowers and have the vines in their bright autumn colors coming down over the cloth. Little baskets to match the center basket filled with bonbons may be at each plate, with a tiny bouquet or a single blossom tied to the handles.

A rustic basket filled with daisies makes a delightful centerpiece, or a daisy-ball can be suspended from the light fixtures over the table, with daisy chains reaching from it to each plate, where there may be small baskets of daisies. One flower, such as an iris, is often effective in a basket or small vase. One of these could be placed at each plate and two or three in the center of the table or one each at the ends and one in the center. One can procure odd-shaped and unique baskets that certain flowers will be at their best in. Lilacs will look pretty in a green basket, as will also pink roses. Daffodils, jonquils, pansies, valley lilies, or any short-stemmed flowers look best in shallow baskets or vases and arranged as if growing. A pretty effect may be obtained by filling a long narrow basket with some of these short-stemmed blossoms and using as a centerpiece—a basket about one foot by two would do very nicely.

A shower of valley lilies and pink rosebuds suspended over the table is very effective. Use pale green ribbons to tie the stems to; or a bunch of American beauty roses and valley lilies tied together into a loose bouquet with tulle ribbon and placed at intervals over the table makes a charming effect. Another pretty effect is to use a heart-shaped wreath for the centerpiece made of flowers and vines; this may either be placed flat on the table or suspended from the light fixtures by tulle, as desired.

For pink and white effects, pink roses and white hyacinth with asparagus ferns makes a pretty centerpiece, arranged in a fancy green basket or in a pretty bowl. If a basket with a handle is used tulle ribbon may be tied to the handle; spirea and asparagus ferns make another good combination. The trailing arbutus may be used with its own foliage. Pink and white sweet peas are nice combined, and a little of their own foliage may be used.

On the ribbons of the table, on the tulle, baskets of flowers and candies may be tiny figures of cupids, or tiny hearts can be used. A very pretty effect is obtained by making a mat of smilax and ferns in the center of the table and sticking pansies here and there over it, or any small short-stemmed blossoms; these will have the effect as if growing. If you have plenty of flowers you can arrange a broad plateau of flowers the entire length of the table.

The wedding-cake may very appropriately be used as a centerpiece; in this case it should be a decorated cake. The cake may rest on a wreath of ferns, or be encircled with a wreath of flowers. Candied violets, rose petals, candied citron, lemon and orange rind and angelica are all well adapted for decorating the wedding-cake, also candied cherries and little candies. Icing can also be arranged in fanciful designs.

MENUS FOR THE WEDDING BREAKFASTS OR LUNCHEONS

Green and White

Pineapple Relish

Spinach Bouillon   Wafers
   White Radishes   Olives
    Lamb Chops Garnished with Parsley
          Rolls
Peas in White Sauce   Potato Soufflé
     Pistachio Nut Salad
Lemon-Ice   Cakes Iced in White and Green
    Green and White Mints

Cream of Pea Soup
   Cucumbers   Olives
    Chicken Cutlets with Asparagus Sauce
Rice Balls   Lettuce Sandwiches
    Cabbage and Nut Salad
  Mint Sherbet   Angel Food Cake
    Salted Pistachio Nuts

Gold and White

Grapefruit Cup Topped with White Grapes
Whitefish Cutlets with Olive Sauce   Hot Rolls
   Chicken Breast in Yellow Aspic
    Potato Cheese Balls
Banana and Pineapple or Peach Salad   Wafers
  Ice-Cream   Bride's Cake
   Yellow and White Bonbons

Gold and Green

Orange Mint Relish

Olives   Celery Hearts
Cream of Clam Soup with Whipped Cream
Lamb Chops or Veal Cutlets   Minced Buttered Carrots
Sweet Potato Croquettes
Egg and Lettuce Salad
Pistachio Cream   Orange Cakes
Mint Macaroons

Red and Gold

Grapefruit with Halved Strawberries or Maraschino Cherries
Cream Consommé   Bread Sticks
Red and Yellow Radishes
Roast Lamb with Cherry Sauce   Pimiento Sandwiches
Creamed Beets   Scalloped Potatoes
Tomato Salad
Strawberry Ice-Cream   Sunshine Cake

Red and White

Red Raspberries
Baked Whitefish with Tomato Sauce   Chicken Croquettes
Hot Biscuits   Strawberry Preserves
Corn in Tomato Cups   Creamed Potatoes
Bean and Beet Salad   Cheese Wafers
Cherry and Pineapple Dessert
Assorted Cakes

Pink and White

Cherry Appetizer

Deviled Lobster in Shells   Pimiento Sandwiches

Pink and White Radishes

Chicken Timbales   Potato Balls (with pink sauce)

Cottage Cheese Salad

Strawberry or Red Raspberry Whip or Mousse

Glacé Currants (pink and white)

Cocoanut Cake

Pink and White Bonbons

Rose Menu

Rose Bouillon (cream bouillon colored with lobster coral)

Rose Sandwiches

Lemon Jelly Molds (with rosebud in center)

Lobster Cutlets

Rose Potatoes   Radish Roses

Rose Sherbet   Wild Rose Cakes

Candied Rose Petals   Marshmallow Roses

Purple and White

Grape Juice Cocktail in White Cups

Fried Fillets of Fish   Cauliflower Pickle

Chicken in Aspic

Baked Eggplant   Mushrooms in Pastry Shells

Jellied Fruit Salad

Grape Juice Charlotte

Cake Decorated with Candied Violets

Purple and White Bonbons

Salted Pistachio Nuts

WEDDING RECEPTION MENUS

Menu No. 1

Chicken in Pastry Shells   Assorted Sandwiches
Surprise Croquettes
Olives   Sweet Pickles
Pineapple-Ice   White Fruit Wedding Cake
Salted Almonds

Menu No. 2

Chicken Croquettes   Rolls
Olives   Spiced Fruit
Lobster Salad
Cream Puffs   Angel Food Cake
Bonbons

Menu No. 3

Hot Crisp Rolls   Fish in Ramekins
Sweetbreads in Cucumber Jelly Cups
Olives   Radishes
Strawberry or Raspberry Ice-Cream
Lady Baltimore Cake
Bonbons   Salted Nuts

Menu No. 4

Sliced Turkey Loaf   Assorted Sandwiches
Salmon in Aspic
Pickled Beets   Cucumbers
Nut and Cheese Salad
Orange Sticks
Assorted Cakes   Marshmallow Parfait
Bonbons

CHICKEN BREAST IN YELLOW ASPIC

1 pint stock

1 bay leaf

½ teaspoonful Worcester-
shire

½ cupful mayonnaise

½ ounce gelatin

1 teaspoonful onion-juice

2 or 3 cloves

Salt and pepper

3 egg-yolks

¼ cupful chopped celery

Place the stock in a double boiler with the bay leaf, cloves, and let simmer a little while, then remove and stir in the onion-juice, salt and pepper and the gelatin which should have soaked in one-half cupful of water for an hour or so. Add the mayonnaise, the yolks of the hard-boiled eggs rubbed into a paste, and the chopped celery. Place bits of the white chicken breast in a mold and pour the aspic around it. Chill and turn out onto a pretty plate when ready to serve.

POTATO CHEESE BALLS

1 cupful mashed potatoes

⅛ teaspoonful mustard

3 eggs

1 cupful grated cream cheese

Dash of cayenne

Cracker crumbs

Mix the grated cheese into the mashed potatoes and season, adding salt to taste, and the other seasoning as given. Mold into balls about the size of walnuts after the stiffly-beaten whites of the eggs have been folded in. Roll in cracker crumbs rolled very fine and fry in deep fat a golden brown.

ORANGE-MINT RELISH

½ dozen oranges	1 pineapple
½ cupful powdered sugar	2 tablespoonfuls mint
1 tablespoonful lemon-juice	1 tablespoonful pineapple-juice
Crystallized mint	

Remove the skin and the bitter part from the oranges and cut up into bits. Peel the pineapple, slice and cut into cubes. Mix the two fruits together, then sprinkle with the sugar and add the mint chopped very fine and the fruit-juices. Let stand on ice for an hour or so before serving. Serve in sherbet glasses or lemonade glasses. Garnish with mint.

CHERRY SAUCE

1 pint cherries	1 pint water
Cloves and allspice	Mint
1 lemon	2 tablespoonfuls butter
Pinch of salt	2 tablespoonfuls flour

Place the cherries and water together and

cook until tender; then pass through a sieve. Blend the butter and flour together, add the salt and stir in the cherry purée. The spices should be simmered with the cherries, while the mint should not be added until the last thing. Cook until smooth and thick, stirring constantly. Serve with the lamb.

Strawberry Whip or Mousse

1 pint strawberry-pulp   1 quart cream
Sugar

Take some nice ripe strawberries and mash into a pulp. Beat the cream up very stiff. Sweeten the pulp, then fold in the cream and pour into a mold and pack in ice and salt for several hours. Turn out when ready to serve, slice and garnish each slice with whole berries.

Rose Potatoes

Round potatoes   Hot fat

Peel the potatoes, and peel round and round as though peeling to the core. To do this use a very thin and narrow-bladed knife to keep from breaking the continuous peel. Place in ice-cold water, slightly salted, and let stand an hour, drain and fry in boiling hot fat as you would Saratoga chips. Form into roses, and serve on lettuce leaves.

ROSE SHERBET

1 cupful orange-juice	1 quart strawberry-juice
1 cupful pineapple-juice	1 pint water
2 cupfuls sugar	1 tablespoonful gelatin
3 eggs	Strawberry extract or rose

Mix the juice and sugar together and dissolve the gelatin in a little cold water and stir into the pint of water heated to the boiling point; add this to the fruit-juices, and add the extract. Pour into a freezer and freeze until mushy, then stir in the stiffly beaten white of eggs. If not a rose color add enough red fruit coloring to make a rose shade.

GRAPE-JUICE COCKTAIL

1 pint grape-juice	1 cupful orange-pulp
1 cupful pineapple	Sugar

Mix the fruits together and sprinkle with sugar; then arrange in glasses and pour the grape-juice over them. The pineapple and oranges should be cut up into rather large pieces.

GRAPE-JUICE CHARLOTTE

Grape-juice sherbet   Sponge cup cakes

Freeze some grape-juice as you would for other sherbets, adding a little pineapple or lemon-juice, if liked. Hollow the sponge cup-cakes out and fill with the grape sherbet. Garnish with nuts or candied violets.

SURPRISE CROQUETTES

Follow any recipe for rice croquettes, but when molding into balls or cones, tuck a bit of preserved fruit in the center of each, or a bit of nut. Roll in cracker or bread-crumbs and beaten egg and fry in deep fat like other croquettes.

SALMON IN ASPIC

1 pint clear stock   1 can pink salmon
1 tablespoonful lemon-   ½ ounce gelatin
   juice   Salt and paprika
Bay leaf and a clove or two

Make an aspic with the stock and gelatin. Simmer the spices in the stock several minutes and then remove. Dissolve the gelatin in a little cold water and stir into the hot stock. Season. When the stock begins to jelly pour one-half into the mold, then add the salmon, and pour over the remainder of the stock. Chill and turn out when ready to serve. The pink fish showing through the clear aspic makes a very pretty dish.

MARSHMALLOW PARFAIT

1 quart water	2 cupfuls sugar
2 cupfuls orange-juice	¼ cupful lemon-juice
1 dozen marshmallows	Pinch of salt
Orange extract	

Place the sugar and water in a saucepan and bring to the boiling point. Place the marshmallows on top of this and cover and let stand until soft; then beat up, add the fruit-juices and extract. Cool and freeze. Serve in tall glasses.

POTATO SOUFFLÉ

½ dozen large potatoes	1 tablespoonful butter
½ cupful cream	3 eggs
Salt and pepper	

Cook or bake the potatoes until tender, then

mash up or pass through a potato ricer; add the butter, milk and seasoning and beat up; then fold in the stiffly beaten whites of the eggs. Pour into bake-dish and bake until puffed up and a nice brown. Serve hot in the dish in which it has been baked.

OLIVE SAUCE FOR FISH

2 tablespoonfuls butter	3 tablespoonfuls flour
1 slice onion	1 cupful water
½ cupful soup stock	½ cupful chopped olives
Salt and pepper	1 tablespoonful lemon-juice

Place the butter in a double boiler and add the onion, chopped very fine and brown; then stir in the flour and when well-blended stir in the water and stock heated to the boiling point. Stir until smooth; then add the chopped olives, the lemon-juice and the salt and pepper and a little paprika. A tablespoonful of chopped pimiento will add to this sauce for many.

WEDDING CAKES

The trimming of a wedding-cake adds much to its appearance. In making the cake you can follow any of the recipes given and then decorate. A very pretty decoration for a wedding-cake is to cut hearts out of slices of angel food cake, dip these in pink or red fondant. In the center of these angel food hearts place hearts cut out of candied cherries, if the hearts have been dipped in pink fondant. Ice the cake in white, and while the icing is still soft arrange these little hearts all around the sides of the cake and on top, or one larger than the rest may be used on the top.

Wild roses may be cut out of these thin slices of angel food cake, dipped in rose-colored fondant. Place a drop of chocolate or yellow fondant in the center of each. Arrange these on top of the cake; the leaves may be made in the same manner, dipped in leaf-green fondant flavored with pistachio and veined with yellow fondant or chocolate. Arrange these using angelica for stems.

Fondant may be piped onto cakes to form almost any design or flower wished. Little heart-shaped candies on which are lettered sentimental verses are nice to decorate wedding and bridal-cakes. Candied rose petals may be cut out and formed into rosebuds and flowers, and a wreath of these with angelica or citron leaves can be easily arranged on the cake, with a little painstaking care. One can obtain all sorts of candy mites and flat mints with which a wedding-cake may be decorated.

TABLE IDEAS FOR ANNOUNCEMENT LUNCHEONS

The cat-out-of-the-bag idea may be very cleverly carried out in the following manner: From the lights over the table suspend a pretty bag made out of Dresden or flowered ribbon; or if preferred the bag may be made out of crepe paper in some pretty flower design, or some delicate shade. The top of the bag may be kept open by means of an embroidery hoop. This bag should be filled with pretty blossoms that are in season, and from amidst the flowers should peep out a wise-looking pussy-cat, which may be of china, papier-mâché or stiff paper.

At each plate have a little paper bag with a cat's head protruding. At the close of the luncheon, when the guests pull out the cats they find attached to them little heart-shaped cards on which are written the names of the engaged couple.

THE SECRET IN THE TRUNK

A unique method of announcing an engagement is by means of miniature trunks placed at each plate. The trunk at the bride-to-be's plate should contain a ring and a tiny red heart, while the others may contain tiny cupids bearing a card on which is written the name of the fortunate gentleman.

The centerpiece for the table may be a heart-shaped wreath, fastened upright to a pasteboard foundation, which should be cleverly concealed with flowers and ferns. The wreath may be made of fine wire, covered with green crepe paper, then with small blossoms. From the center of this wreath should swing a cupid.

If preferred the centerpiece may be a miniature bride and groom all dressed ready for a bridal journey; they may be standing beside a miniature railroad depot, suggesting a wedding trip. On the depot platform there might be a number of toy trunks.

After the final course, a small trunk, filled with rose petals, is passed and each guest takes a handful and showers the bride-elect.

The cake may be baked to represent a trunk, iced with a maple icing, and the straps marked on with chocolate. Use strips of candied orange peel for the handles and letter the name of the bride-elect on the top with tiny candies. Tie tiny hearts to the handles.

A Bouquet Announcement Table

A unique and charming method of announcing an engagement is to conceal the names of the engaged couple in the hearts of tiny bouquets held by dolls dressed to represent bridesmaids. There should be one of these at each plate. For a centerpiece have a miniature bride and groom standing on a heart made of ferns and delicate vines or moss. Decorate the place-cards with little bouquets of flowers, either done in water colors or appliqued on. A novel idea is to serve ice-cream cones in the center of bouquets; these should be placed in vases in which there is no water, of course; or if you prefer you can serve the bonbons in cones made of cardboard or pasteboard and inserted in the center of bouquets.

The names of the engaged couple may be simply written on slips of paper and inserted in the center of the bouquets or else tiny heart-shaped cards can be used for this purpose. Have a little end of ribbon sticking out to give the guests a hint of what the bouquet contains.

CHERRY AND STRAWBERRY SHOWER LUNCHEON

Rolls   Radishes   Strawberry Preserves
        Lobster Patties   Strawberry Salad
              Strawberry Sherbet
Cocoanut Cakes   Strawberry Bonbons

Tomato Bouillon

Rolls   Cherry Preserves
            Lamb Chops with Cherry Sauce
        Cherry Salad   Creamed Beets
Cherry Gelatin Pudding   Cherry Cakes
            Cherry Bonbons

These luncheons are nice to give to a bride-elect when showering her with strawberry or cherry preserves and jellies.

The table for the cherry luncheon may be exquisitely decorated with twigs, with the leaves and clusters of the fruit upon them; there are not only the red cherries, but the yellow and pink-tinted cherries, and also the " black hearts." These may be arranged on the white table-cloth, and a pretty vase holding several twigs may serve as a centerpiece. At each plate have pretty glasses of delicious amber-hued cherry preserves; these are presented to the bride-to-be after the luncheon. The bride-elect may also be given a booklet decorated with cherries done in water colors. Each leaf should contain a recipe for preserving and serving the fruit and signed by the contributor. The cherry bonbons may be served in cherry-decorated boxes, and the place-cards should be decorated with cherries.

The strawberry idea may be carried out by placing in the center of the table a low fern receptacle filled with strawberry vines with their bright red berries and blossoms. Plants having large clusters of berries and a few blossoms should be chosen for this purpose. At each plate have a little raffia basket filled with large strawberries with the stems left on. Strawberry leaves may be carelessly scattered here and there over the table-cloth. At the bride-elect's plate there should be a dainty little cook-book, the covers decorated with cupids and hearts. This book should contain recipes for preserving strawberries and also for other ways of serving the fruit, contributed by the guests.

Have tiny jars of strawberry preserves at each plate to be eaten with the rolls. The place-cards may be decorated with a few leaves of strawberries done in water colors. The favors may be little strawberry emerys. The strawberry bonbons should be served in little baskets. If candles are used have white candles with pink shades.

A CLOVER SHOWER LUNCHEON

Chicken Patties   Sandwiches
                Red and White Radishes
        Tomato Salad   Cherry Tarts
Whole Strawberries   Ice-Cream
                    Clover Cakes
                Green and Pink Mints

This is really a linen shower, but the designs on the linen should be in clover-leaf design and the embroidered pieces may all be done in clover designs. The decoration of the house and table should be in clover blossoms and leaves. Have for the centerpiece of the table a low rustic basket filled with clover-blossoms, and leaves as if growing. Delicate trails of clover-leaves and blossoms should extend from each corner of the basket to the corners of the table and here attached to small horseshoes of clover-blossoms. At each plate have little enameled wheelbarrows filled with home-made bonbons and the top decorated with a mass of clover-blossoms. The place-cards may be decorated with pressed clover leaves; the ones on the bride-elect's card being the lucky four-leaved clovers, while those on the others may be the common trefoils. If candles are used have them creamy white with pink shades. Decorate the ice-cream with four-leaved clovers cut out of crystallized mint. The strawberries should be served in little baskets enameled white—a creamy white. Serve the radishes on green glass plates.

The pieces of linen should be placed in boxes decorated with four-leaved clovers.

A Rose Shower Luncheon

Any bride-to-be whose home is to be a suburban one will be delighted with a rose shower. Each girl is asked to bring a rose-bush. Of course, these are in pots all ready to be set out when convenient. The dining-room can be beautifully decorated with roses. Full-blown roses can be tied rather loosely on a strong cord and the result will be a number of ropes of roses which are festooned about the frieze of the room. Roses are also arranged about the rooms in bowls and baskets. The center-piece for the table should be a large bouquet of roses, and across the table have drifted rose-petals. At each plate have a single rosebud to which is attached a small cardboard heart, bearing an appropriate quotation. A few suitable quotations are given below:

When we should live together in a cozy little cot,
Hid in a nest of roses, with a fairy-garden spot,
Where the vines were ever fruited and the weather ever
fine
And the birds were ever singing for that old sweetheart
of mine.

—RILEY.

What glory then for me,
In such company?
Roses plenty, roses plenty,
And one nightingale for twenty.
—ELIZABETH BROWNING.

Jasmine is sweet and has many loves,
And the broom's bethrothed to the bee;
But I will plight with the dainty rose,
For fairest of all is she.
                                    —HOOD.

'Tis said as Cupid danced among
The gods, he down the nectar flung,
Which on the white rose being shed
Made it ever after red.
                                    —HERRICK.

For there the rose, o'er crag and vale,
Sultana of the nightingale,
The maid for whom his melody,
His thousand songs are heard on high,
Blooms blushing, to her lover's tale.
                                    —BYRON.

Flowers of all hues, and without thorn, the rose.—MILTON.

The refreshments can consist of lobster-patties, creamed peas served in pretty white paper cases, edged with pink; tomatoes with mayonnaise, served on lettuce leaves; pink ice-cream, which can be served in little earthen pots with a rose sticking in each, the top covered with grated chocolate to represent earth; cakes, iced in pink, and chocolate, with whipped cream tinted pink, on top.

The menu given for a rose luncheon under wedding receptions may be very appropriately used.

A BASKET SHOWER

The invitation cards can be decorated with little baskets of flowers cut out of post-cards and appliqued on, then the edges touched up with gilt. The rooms should be charmingly decorated with baskets of flowers. Grape and other fruit baskets can be enameled in pink and white. The pink baskets can be filled with white flowers while the white baskets should be filled with pink blossoms; these baskets can be suspended here and there about the rooms by means of ribbon to harmonize or placed on stands, mantels and so on.

The bride-elect is showered with baskets, large and small. First might come two of the guests with a large clothes-basket or hamper filled with spring blossoms. On investigation it is found to be nearly full of small kitchen utensils bought at the five and ten-cent stores, pink paper, and on top of the pink paper the flowers are placed; then the next should be a market basket filled with all sorts of queer packages, a work basket, all fitted out ready for "the stitch in time," a waste-basket with flaring top, filled with pink and white roses, a hanging-basket containing an aspara-gus fern or oxalis, and one or two fancy little baskets which contain handkerchiefs and towels or anything preferred. Last of all she should be showered with little crepe paper baskets filled with blossoms—each guest throwing one at her simultaneously.

The centerpiece for the table can be a fancy basket made out of raffia or paper rope, or can be a boughten one, in delicate green and filled with pink and white rosebuds and delicate ferns. Pink and white sweet peas could be used instead of the rosebuds. At the guests' plates have smaller baskets filled with pink and white rosebuds or sweet peas, from the handles of which can be suspended tiny gilt hearts. White candles with pink shades, edged with a row of gilt hearts, will add to the effect. Pink and white bonbons can be served in little baskets made out of paper rope in delicate green, the edges of which can be touched up with gilt paint.

The refreshments can be almost entirely served from baskets. The sandwiches can be served from a low basket, the edge decorated with rosebuds and ferns. Creamed chicken can be served in little pastry-baskets, and the salad in little baskets made of lettuce leaves. The ices are served in little green baskets, the top decorated with candied flowers, and the angel food cake can be iced in white and decorated with pink candy hearts bearing little sentimental verses.

A SPRINGTIME LUNCHEON FOR A BRIDE-ELECT

Green, the color of spring, should be used as the color scheme, except for the touch of pink for the bride-elect, which is the novel feature of the luncheon. Foliage plants, ferns and trailing vines from the woods, with a few white hyacinths and lilies-of-the-valley can be used in decorating the rooms. A mat of ferns is arranged in the center of the table and on this is placed a white basket filled with maiden-hair ferns, white hyacinths and lilies-of-the-valley. At the bride-elect's plate is a small bouquet of pink rosebuds tied together with narrow green ribbon. At the other places are small bouquets of the valley lilies. The honor guest's chair is marked by a wreath of pink flowers tied to the back with green maline. The heart-shaped place-cards are cut out of pale green cardboard, except the bride-elect's card, which is of pink cardboard decorated with a tiny cupid.

The green-and-white idea, with the touch of pink for the bride-elect, is carried out in the refreshments served. The lettuce sandwiches are rolled, a few tied with pink ribbon, the rest with green ribbon. Sweetbreads, garnished with asparagus tips, are served in paper cases made by covering plain cases with white crepe paper and tinting the edges pale green, except the bride's which is pink. The salad is made from the white meat of the chicken, celery and chopped olives, with a white mayonnaise dressing. The portion served to the honor guest is on pink rose petals. The green mints are served in white paper rose-cases. White vanilla ice-cream in heart-shape is served on white plates wreathed with smilax and the bride-to-be's with pink rosebuds and smilax. The angel food cake is cut into squares, iced in white, then decorated with green candy hearts; the bride-elect's with tiny pink heart-shaped candies. Green and white candles are used. The guest of honor is showered with packages done up in pink, white and green.

MENUS FOR ANNOUNCEMENT LUNCHEONS

Grapefruit Cup Topped with Maraschino Cherries
Chicken Cutlets
Stuffed Red Peppers
(served on heart-shaped pieces of bread)
Heart-shaped Biscuit   Strawberry Preserves
Sweetbread Tomato Salad (served on Lettuce Leaves)
Ice Cream in Heart-shaped Cases   Pink Heart Cakes
Heart-shaped Bonbons

Tomato Bouillon
Quail on Heart-shaped Pieces of Toast
Potato Chips   Hot Rolls   Currant Jelly
Cucumber Salad in Lettuce Cups
Ice-Cream in Heart-shape with Strawberry Sauce
Salted Almonds   Little Cakes

Menus for Spring Luncheons
Cream Bouillon with Bread-sticks
Scalloped Scallops and Mushrooms in
Heart-shaped Ramekins
Veal Fillets   Rice Croquettes
String Bean Salad
Vanilla Mousse with Strawberries   Cocoanut Cake

Cherry Cup
Chicken Sandwiches   Currant Sandwiches
Baked Stuffed Cucumbers
Lettuce and Asparagus Salad   Wafers
Strawberry Ice-Cream
Assorted Cakes   Bonbons

SCALLOPED SCALLOPS AND MUSHROOMS

1 pint scallops   1 cupful mushrooms
1 cupful cracker crumbs 2 tablespoonfuls butter
1 cupful milk   1 tablespoonful flour
Salt and pepper

Make a cream sauce with the butter, flour
and milk, season to taste, then stir in the mush-

rooms and cook a few minutes. Place in the bottom of a bake-dish a layer of crackers, pour in a little mushroom cream sauce, then add half of the scallops, then a layer of cream sauce, then the remainder of the scallops. Cover with cracker-crumbs and bake in the oven for about twenty minutes or until a nice brown on top and the scallops are cooked.

BAKED STUFFED CUCUMBERS

Cucumbers (large)	1 cupful bread-crumbs
1 cupful chopped chicken	1 slice bacon
1 egg	1 teaspoonful parsley
1 tablespoonful butter	Salt and pepper

Take large cucumbers and peel and halve; scoop out all the seeds. Mix the bread-crumbs and the chopped cooked chicken, shred the fried bacon up into small bits, and add; season and moisten with the beaten egg and the butter (melted). Fill the cavities with this. Place in a bake-pan with a little water and bake for forty or more minutes, or until the cucumbers are nice and tender. Place each half on a plate and garnish with watercress or parsley.

TABLE DECORATIONS FOR WEDDING ANNIVERSARIES

The wedding anniversaries which are most frequently celebrated are the paper wedding, cotton wedding, the wooden wedding, the tin wedding, crystal wedding, china wedding, silver wedding and golden wedding. Occasionally the ruby, pearl and diamond weddings are celebrated.

Wedding anniversaries are popular events, worthy of being celebrated in our very best manner. Under each wedding anniversary menus are given for luncheon, dinner or supper.

THE PAPER WEDDING

It will be quite easy to plan for a paper wedding anniversary table in this day when one is able to get crepe paper in such amazing variety, both in richness and coloring, and in unique and interesting designs. The texture of this paper lends itself to every shape and fancy of decoration.

If you wish something simple yet effective in way of table decorations use odd-shaped baskets woven with crepe paper rope, making these as you would raffia baskets. They may be made or procured in any shade desired; but the dark shades will prove most effective, although very pretty color effects may be obtained with the paler shades. A pale green basket is pretty filled with pale pink or with white flowers. A pale yellow basket filled with blue or white flowers also makes a pretty color scheme. A dark green basket filled with deep red roses makes a striking and charming centerpiece, or a brown basket with yellow blossoms, or a dull blue basket with white or yellow blossoms.

Cute little bonbon holders to match the basket in the center of the table may also be made of this paper rope. Fill these with kisses or caramels wrapped in waxed paper. Paper cases made in form of lettuce or cabbage heads are nice in which to serve salads and ices. Use waxed paper to line these cases.

The new paper applique work is nice to use for the table decorations for this anniversary. Passe-partout paper in different colors is used for the applique work. Designs are cut out of this gummed paper and applied upon place-cards, bonbon boxes, ice cups, paper plates, lamp shades and such like. Color schemes may be nicely carried out in this way, using blue and white, pink and white, green and white and such like schemes. The designs may be conventional or may be applied to form scenes, people and so forth.

PAPER WEDDING MENUS

Luncheon Menu

Assorted Sandwiches

Green Salad in Paper Lettuce Cases

Creamed Peas in Paper Cabbage Cups

Strawberry or Cherry Sherbet in Paper Rose Cases

Little Cakes with Paper Frills

Bonbons Wrapped in Delicate Shades of Crepe Paper

Dinner Menu

Cream of Corn Soup

Creamed Fish in Paper Cases

Olives   Pickled Cucumbers

Lamb Chops with Paper Frills

Creamed Potatoes in Paper Ramekins

Hot Rolls

Tomato Salad (served on a lettuce leaf on paper plates)

Ice-Cream in Paper Cases

Assorted Cakes   Bonbons

Supper Menu

Sandwiches (wrapped in waxed paper)   Marguerites

Stuffed Olives

Oyster or Chicken Salad (in paper cases)

Ice-Cream in Paper Cases   Lord Baltimore Cake

Caramels

TABLE DECORATIONS FOR THE COTTON WEDDING

The decorations for a cotton wedding should be in white except for a touch of green. Snowballs make a pretty decoration if flowers are to be used, or any white blossoms may be used. Place the white bowl on a mat made of cotton and sprinkled heavily with diamond dust or mica. The most effective decorations for a cotton wedding are balls of cotton batting, sprinkled with diamond dust, placed on a cotton mat or on a mat of ferns. A plate of popcorn balls rolled in rock candy, chopped up, also makes an appropriate centerpiece. If you have access to cotton-plants, have cotton balls at each plate, or these could be made. The place-cards may be made of cotton cloth with the names lettered on.

Pretty baskets made of cretonne or pretty flowered goods of some kind could be filled with ferns and flowers, and smaller baskets or boxes could be used for the bonbons.

MENUS FOR THE COTTON WEDDING

· Luncheon

Assorted Sandwiches   White Chicken Salad
Cottage Cheese Molded in form of Cotton Bales
Potato Balls with White Sauce
Pineapple Snowballs   Angel Food Cake
Cotton Candy

Dinner Menu

Clam Bouillon with Whipped Cream
Creamed Whitefish in Pastry Shells   Pickled Onions
Roast Chicken or Veal
Riced Potatoes   Creamed Turnips
Orange Salad Topped with White Grapes
Cocoanut Snowballs   Cotton Bales (Cakes)
Cocoanut Cubes   Popcorn Balls

Supper Menu

Hot Fluffy Biscuits   Pear Preserves

White Fruit Salad

Creamed Chicken in Rice Cups   Pickled Cauliflower

Cocoanut Macaroons

TABLE DECORATIONS FOR THE WOODEN WEDDING

It is best to leave the dining-room table without a cover, using only a few mats, since you will wish to show as much wood as possible. The centerpiece may be a pretty rustic basket filled with wildwood beauties; or a woven willow-basket filled with red blossoms of some sort. A little birch-bark boat filled with water lilies would be charming. The place-cards may be birch-bark or thin cards of wood with the names burnt in with a needle. Wooden plates should be used and these may be decorated with pressed ferns and flowers gummed around the edge; or pretty designs cut from post-cards or magazines. Cover the plates with waxed paper. Delightful little wooden nut-bowls may be obtained to hold the nuts and bonbons. The wooden Dutch shoes or little pails are nice in which to serve salads and such like. Line these with waxed paper before placing the food in them.

Since wood alone gives a dull tone to a table it is well to introduce a touch of red into both the table decorations and menus. A wooden bowl filled with red blossoms would make a harmonious centerpiece, and at each end of the table might be wooden bowls of rosy red apples or other red fruits. The candies may be red and will look nice in the little wooden receptacles.

Wooden Wedding Menus

Luncheon Menu

Baked Bean Sandwiches   Chocolate Sandwiches
Tomato Salad on Wooden Plates
Spiced Pears
Chocolate Pudding with Maple Sauce
Cake Iced to Represent Wood
(Iced with Maple Icing and Grained with Chocolate)
Maple and Chocolate Bonbons   Salted Nuts

Dinner Menu

Tomato Bouillon

Stuffed Baked Fish with Brown Sauce

Stuffed Parker House Rolls   Spiced Peaches

Roast Beef with Brown Sauce

Baked Beans in Wooden Bowls

Salad in Wooden Pails   Browned Potatoes

Pickled Beets on Wooden Plates

Strawberries in Pails   Little Cakes

Chocolate Macaroons   Nuts

Supper Menu

Brown Bread Sandwiches

Rice Croquettes with Cheese Sauce

Salad in Wooden Receptacles

Chocolate Ice-Cream in Wooden Cases

Chocolate Almonds   Maple Caramel Cake

Candies

CHOCOLATE PUDDING WITH MAPLE SAUCE

4 eggs	½ cupful sugar
2 cupfuls scalded milk	2 ounces chocolate (melted)
1 cupful whipped cream	½ cupful figs
1 teaspoonful vanilla	½ cupful dates
½ cupful water	Maple sauce

Beat the yolks of the eggs up well, then add the sugar; stir in gradually the scalded milk, then the unsweetened chocolate. Put in a double boiler and stir until it thickens and coats the spoon. Let stand until cold, then stir in the whipped cream, pour into a freezer. Cut the figs and dates up fine, or pass through a food chopper and add one-fourth cupful sugar to the water and add the fruit and cook until tender, flavor with vanilla. When the cream is almost done, stir in the stiffly-beaten whites of the eggs and the fruit mixture which should be cold, and finish freezing. When done place in a mold and let stand for an hour or so packed in ice and salt.

To make the maple sauce place in a double boiler one cupful of water, one-half cupful maple sirup or sugar and a pinch of salt; when it comes to a boil stir in one tablespoonful of corn-starch that has been blended in one-fourth cupful cream. Stir until smooth and thick, add a small pinch of cinnamon. Let cool before pouring around the frozen pudding when served.

THE TIN WEDDING

Use only the bright new tin. Tinware may

be made quite decorative by enameling the outside in white or in delicate shades and stenciling on them conventional designs, or passepartout paper may be applied in decorative effect on white or delicately tinted backgrounds. If liked this can be gone over with clear varnish. Delightful effects may be obtained in this way, and one would scarcely be aware that the food was being served from tin utensils.

The centerpiece for the table may be formed of two tin funnels by placing the two small ends together; this makes a unique centerpiece that may be filled with flowers and ferns. A tin water-pot, or a tin seaside pail are also possibilities. Small toy horns filled with flowers or bonbons may be found at each plate.

New pie-tins may serve as plates, and tin-cups may be used for the coffee. Creamed chicken, peas, corn or potatoes may be served in small tin toy tubs or pails; these may also be used in which to serve salads if they are first lined with waxed paper. Heart-shaped jelly molds are nice for this purpose. The place-cards may be heart-shaped bits of tin, which

the tinsmith will cut out for you. Paint the
names on these.

Tin Wedding Menus

Luncheon Menu

Cream Consommé in Small Tin Cups
Stuffed Rolls
Cheese Soufflé Baked in Tin Pudding Pan and Served in It
Creamed Peas in Individual Tin Tubs
Salad Served in Individual Tin Molds

Meringue Mousse   White Cakes
Bonbons   Nuts

Dinner Menu

Mushroom Soup in Tin Cups   Panned Clams
Stuffed Olives   Sweet Pickles
Roast Chicken or Turkey
Scalloped Potatoes
(served in tin-pan in which they are baked)
Hot Muffins (served in tin-pans in which they are baked)
Strawberry Preserves
Salad (served in individual tin-tubs)   Cheese Wafers
Prune Soufflé (served in tin pudding-pan)
Cake   Candies

Supper Menu

Clam Bouillon in Tin-cups   Wafers
Creamed Chicken or Oysters in Tin Molds
Sandwiches
Molded Fruit Salad   Assorted Cakes

MERINGUE MOUSSE

6 eggs   1 teaspoonful almond
2 cupfuls water   extract
2 cupfuls of sugar   1 quart whipped cream

Beat up the whites of the eggs very stiff. Make a thick sirup with the water and sugar, boiling it until it spins a thread. Place the egg-whites in a dish and pour the hot sirup over them and beat up until light and foamy, add the almond extract and carefully fold in the whipped cream, when the egg mixture is cool enough. Pour into a mold and pack in ice and salt and let stand for several hours. This is nice served with preserved or candied fruits and with fresh fruits also.

PRUNE SOUFFLÉ

1 pound best prunes   ½ cupful sugar
4 eggs   Prune kernels

Wash the prunes well and soak overnight, add the sugar and simmer very slowly until the prunes are tender and plump. Slip out the stones and chop the prunes. Crack the stones, and chop up very fine, and add to the prunes. Beat the whites of the eggs up until stiff, then stir lightly into the prunes. Place in a bake-dish and bake about twenty minutes in a moderate oven. Serve with whipped cream or a sauce.

CHEESE SOUFFLÉ

2 tablespoonfuls butter	2/3 cupful milk
2 tablespoonfuls flour	1 pinch of cayenne
2/3 cupful grated cheese	Salt to taste
3 eggs	

Blend the butter and the flour together in a saucepan, then stir in the milk and season. Cook a few minutes, then stir in the egg-yolks and the cheese. When cool add the stiffly-beaten whites of the eggs. Pour into a buttered bake-dish and bake for about thirty minutes, or until like a custard when done. Serve right from the oven in the dish in which it has been baked.

CREAM OF MUSHROOM SOUP

1 can mushrooms	1 quart chicken stock
1 cupful cream	2 tablespoonfuls butter
Salt and pepper	2 tablespoonfuls flour

Place the stock, water may be used, and the mushrooms in a saucepan and simmer slowly for about thirty minutes. Blend together in a double boiler the butter and the flour and then stir in the cream, stirring constantly until smooth and thick; stir this into the mushrooms. Season to taste and serve with toasted croutons.

FOR THE CRYSTAL WEDDING

The table decorations for the crystal wedding can be made one of the most attractive of all the wedding anniversaries; especially is this so if the wedding-day comes during the summer months, for what can give a more delightfully cool effect than the sparkling crystal? The dining-table should be a picture in sparkling glass. Use this to the exclusion of china as far as practicable.

A pretty centerpiece for a hot summer day would be a square or circular chunk of ice placed on a tray. Pick out a cavity in the center of this block of ice to form a holder for flowers and ferns. Fill the tray with flowers and ferns, also, so as to completely conceal it. If you do not care for the ice centerpiece then you might try the effect produced by placing a tall slender crystal vase on a mirror, concealing the frame with a wreath of flowers. This is very effective.

If artificial light is to be used on the table use white candles in crystal holders, with shades made of frosted crepe paper or paraffine paper. The place-cards may be little squares of isinglass or mica with the names lettered on with green paint. It is nice to introduce a touch of color by using a little colored glass among the clear crystal, for instance the bonbon holders can be pale green filled with rock candy or crystallized fruits, and the relishes may be served on pale green glass plates. Sprays of autumn leaves crystallized with alum or other similar solutions make charming decorations. Crystal icicles may be suspended from the light fixtures.

CRYSTAL WEDDING MENUS

Luncheon Menu

Cream of Salsify Soup
Molded Chicken   Celery Sandwiches
Cucumber Salad
Crystal Dainty   White Cake (with crystallized flowers)
Crystallized Fruits

Dinner Menu

Clear Consommé
Whitefish with Cucumber Jelly   Pickled Onions
Roast Veal   .   Creamed Potatoes
Hot Rolls
Jellied Celery Salad   Cheese Wafers
Jellied Crystallized Fruit Dessert
Rock Candy   Glacé Grapes   Fancy Cakes

Supper Menu

Chicken Sandwiches   Celery Rolls
Grape and Nut Salad
Pineapple Sherbet   Angel Food Cake
Crystallized Fruit   Crystallized Popcorn

Crystal Dainty

3 tablespoonfuls corn-starch

2 lemons

2 eggs

3 cupfuls water

1½ cupfuls sugar

Crystallized pineapple

Dissolve the corn-starch in a little cold water and stir into the water when it has been brought to a boil. Remove from the fire and stir in one tablespoonful butter. Grate the rind and squeeze the juice and stir in the sugar. Add this to the corn-starch, whip in the whites of the stiffly-beaten eggs. Line a mold with crystallized pineapple and turn in the clear corn-starch mixture. Set on ice, turn out and serve with a clear sauce or with whipped cream.

Crystallized Fruit Dessert

Lemon jelly

Crystallized pineapple

Crystallized white grapes

Candied orange-pulp

Make a clear lemon-jelly, following the recipes that come with gelatin. When this begins to set drop in bits of the crystallized fruits. Line the mold also with the fruit and pour in the jelly. Let stand until firm and turn out and serve with whipped cream.

CUCUMBER JELLY FOR FISH

3 large cucumbers
1 slice onion
½ bay leaf
1 pint water
Salt and paprika

1 stalk celery
1 tablespoonful lemon-juice
1 teaspoonful salt (level)
3 tablespoonfuls gelatin

Pare and slice the cucumber and place in a saucepan with the water; then add the stalk of celery, cut into bits, the onion and bay leaf. Simmer slowly until the vegetables are tender, then remove the celery, onion and bay leaf. Pass through a sieve. Dissolve the gelatin in a little cold water and stir into the hot purée. Color pale green with a little spinach-juice or green coloring. Pour into a ring mold. Turn out and heap the fish up in the center of this. If liked no coloring need be added and you will have more of a crystal color. The purée should be seasoned with salt and a dash of paprika and the lemon-juice added.

TABLE DECORATIONS FOR THE CHINA WEDDING

The china wedding may be celebrated in a more formal manner than the ones that have preceded it, and the decorations may be of greater simplicity. Choose the very prettiest china vase, bowl or jardinière you can obtain to hold the flowers—these may be few or many as desired—but should be arranged to harmonize with the rest of the decorations and should be placed where they will give the best effect. The china wedding will give you the chance to display your very best china. If you have any rare old china now is the time to bring it forth.

Use for the centerpiece of the table a pretty china bowl or vase to harmonize with the rest of the china used on the table and fill with blossoms and ferns. It is nice to carry out color schemes with the china, other table decorations and with the menu.

If you wish something more novel in way of table decorations use for a centerpiece two dolls dressed to represent a bride and groom; have the doll dressed in a gown the duplicate of the original wedding-gown. At each plate have small dolls dressed to represent brides-maids; they may be holding tiny bouquets in their hands. The relishes and bonbons may be served in odd-shaped china dishes which may often be picked up at small expense.

China Wedding Menus

Luncheon Menu

Fruit Soup

Lobster Newburg   Chicken Sandwiches

Rice Croquettes

Tomato and Cheese Salad

Ice-Cream   Wafers

Pink and White Macaroons   Cocoanut Cake

Bonbons

Dinner Menu

Cream Consommé

Salmon Loaf with Tomato Sauce

Celery   Spiced Pears

Roast Turkey or Chicken

Creamed Corn in Green Pepper Cases   Creamed Spinach

Cabbage and Nut Salad

Cheese   Crackers

Pistachio Cream   White Fruit Cake

Ginger Creams   Salted Nuts

Supper Menu

Rolls with Chicken Filling   Nut Wafers
          Strips of Veal (breaded)
Salmon and Lemon Jelly Salad
                    Cream Cheese and Pimiento Balls
     Frozen Peaches   Little Cakes
                    Bonbons

LOBSTER NEWBURG

1 pint lobster
½ cupful cream
1 tablespoonful each of
    lemon-juice and sherry

Salt, cayenne, and pinch of
    nutmeg
2 tablespoonfuls butter
2 eggs

Place the butter in a saucepan or chafing-dish, place in the picked lobster and seasoning and heat slowly. Add the lemon-juice and sherry and cook a few moments longer; then add the cream into which has been beaten the yolks of the eggs. Stir until thick.

SALMON LOAF WITH TOMATO SAUCE

1 can salmon
Salt and paprika

1 cupful cooked rice
2 tablespoonfuls butter

Pick all skin and bones from the salmon and mix with the rice into which has been worked the butter. Season to taste with salt and pepper and a dash of paprika or cayenne. Mold into shape of a loaf and bake in the oven a nice brown.

TOMATO SAUCE

1 can tomatoes	2 stalks of celery
1 slice onion	3 sprigs of parsley
1 bay leaf	2 cloves
3 peppercorns	Salt
1 tablespoonful butter	1 tablespoonful flour

Simmer the tomatoes, celery, onion and parsley with spices for twenty minutes. Pass through a sieve. Blend together in a double boiler the flour and butter, then stir in a cupful of tomato purée. Season with salt to taste.

DECORATIONS FOR THE SILVER ANNIVERSARY

Delightful table schemes can be carried out for the silver wedding, which is the one most often celebrated. If you wish something simple, but quite effective, use a silvered basket filled with lilies-of-the-valley or some delicate white blossoms and ferns, or with pink La France roses. This basket may be placed on a silver mat, and mats to match may be placed at each plate, on which place small silvered baskets filled with pink bonbons, or blossoms to match those used in the centerpiece. If you wish something a little more dignified use a silver bowl instead of the basket as the holder for the flowers and ferns.

Use silver candlesticks and as much other silver on the table as good taste suggests. A shower of small silver wedding bells may be suspended from the overhead lights if liked, using silver tinsel to suspend by. The edges of the place-cards should be touched up with silver or be cut out of silvered paper. The ices may be served in little cases made of silvered paper; if liked these may be decorated with little silver bells around the edge.

Have the menu in white in as far as possible, with a touch of green and perhaps pink. Little cakes iced in white with the wedding and anniversary dates put on in tiny silver candies would be nice to serve with pink or white ice-cream.

SILVER WEDDING MENUS

Luncheon Menu

Macédoine of White Fruits

Sweetbread Patties   Rose Sandwiches

Chicken Breast with Asparagus Tips

White Grape and Celery Salad

Pineapple-Ice   Marshmallow Cakes

White and Pink Bonbons

Dinner Menu

Cream of Clam Soup with Whipped Cream

Olives   Mixed Pickles

Creamed Salmon in Patty Shells

Creamed Cauliflower   Potato Balls

Chicken à la Maryland, Rice Balls

Apple and Sweet Pepper Salad

Ice-Cream   Fancy Cakes

Cocoanut Macaroons

Silver Bonbons

Cheese   Crackers

Supper Menu

Salad Sandwiches   Sweet Sandwiches

Veal Croquettes   Potato Chips

Endive Salad   Cheese Wafers

Lemon-Ice   Silver Cake

The Pearl and Ruby Wedding
Anniversaries

The pearl and ruby wedding anniversaries are not so often celebrated as the others; yet there are delightful ideas that can be carried out in the table decorations for such a celebration. Almost perfect imitation of real pearl can be found in beads and fancy ornaments, and one may form unique baskets and holders with these; they should be filled with white roses, sweet peas or other white blossoms and delicate ferns, and should be suspended from the light fixtures over the table where their beauty can be fully seen. A wedding-cake iced in white and decorated with the small pearl-like looking candies that one can obtain would make a nice centerpiece if placed on a mat of pale green and wreathed with white blossoms and ferns, or surrounded with little pearl-colored candles in birthday candle-holders. The place-cards may also be decorated with tiny pearl beads around the edge.

The decorations for the ruby wedding should be in ruby red. Deep red roses in a ruby-colored glass vase can be used for the centerpiece. Use as much ruby-colored glassware on the table as good taste suggests. A deep red basket filled with deep red blossoms could be used for the centerpiece instead of the vase. Small red baskets filled with candied cherries should be at each plate.

PEARL WEDDING MENUS

Luncheon Menu

Cream of Celery Soup   Reception Flakes
          Creamed Corn   Chicken Salad
Hot Biscuits   Quince Honey
                    White Radishes
Pearl Cream   Pearl Cakes
                    White Grapes

Dinner Menu

Clam and Oyster Soup with Whipped Cream
          Creamed Scallops and Mushrooms
White Radishes   Celery
          Chicken Fillets with White Sauce
                    Rice Balls
Stuffed Onions   Scalloped Potatoes
          White Grape Salad   Wafers
Grapefruit Sherbet   Pearl Cake
          Bonbons   Crystallized Pineapple

Supper Menu

Grapefruit Cup Topped with White Grapes

Assorted Sandwiches Jellied Chicken Salad

Hominy Croquettes

Pearl Ice-Cream Little Cakes

Bonbons

SWEETBREAD PATTIES

Pair of sweetbreads

1 cupful rich milk or
  cream

½ dozen oysters

Salt and pepper

1 tablespoonful butter

1 tablespoonful flour

2 tablespoonfuls mush-
  rooms

Pastry

Separate the sweetbreads and parboil in slightly salted water for a half hour, simmering slowly. They should be soaked an hour before parboiling. Separate into small pieces. Blend together in a double boiler one tablespoonful of butter and the same amount of flour; then stir in the rich milk or thin cream and stir until smooth and thick. Season well with salt and pepper; then add the sweetbreads, the oysters and the mushrooms and cook a few minutes longer. Line patty-pans with good puff pastry and bake a nice brown. Fill the creamed sweetbreads into these before serving.

CREAMED SCALLOPS WITH MUSHROOMS

2 cupfuls scallops   ½ cupful cream
½ cupful mushrooms   2 tablespoonfuls flour
Salt and pepper   2 tablespoonfuls butter

Reserve the liquor from about the scallops and add to the milk. Blend the butter and flour together in a double boiler and add the milk and liquor and stir until smooth and thick. Stir in the scallops and the mushrooms and cook for a few minutes; then fill into pastry-shells or serve on bits of toasted bread, cut into fancy shapes. A dash of cayenne may be added.

THE GOLDEN WEDDING ANNIVERSARY

The color scheme for a golden wedding should be carried out in gold-and-white, or blue-and-gold. Yellow roses, tulips, poppies, or any yellow blossoms that are in season can be used. Golden-rod would make nice autumn decorations. Either white, blue or gilded baskets can be used as holders for these blossoms, and used as a centerpiece. As the golden wedding has a dignity of its own there should be a certain simplicity about the affair; but flowers are always appropriate no matter the form of celebration.

Use gold-banded china on the table as far as possible and have gilt-edged cards for place-cards; these would be charming if decorated with the silhouettes of the bride and groom in gold; gold paper could be used for these silhouettes. Small gilded baskets or cornucopias of gilt paper can be at each plate; these should be filled with yellow bonbons. One can obtain pretty gold-lined dishes in which to place the nuts and crystallized fruits. Sherbet or ice-cream can be served in glasses of Bohemian glass; this glass is decorated in gold and adds to the general effect.

GOLDEN WEDDING MENUS

Luncheon Menu

Orange-Ice

Golden Biscuits   Yellow Peach Preserves

Banana Salad

Golden Fish Balls with Hollandaise Sauce   Lemon Tarts

Gold Ring Cakes   Yellow Ice-Cream

Bonbons   Candied Ginger

Dinner Menu

Golden Consommé

Baked Fish with Hollandaise Sauce

Yellow Peach Mangoes Celery Hearts

Fillets of Chicken with Cream Sauce

Glazed Sweet Potatoes Creamed Corn in Carrot Cups

Egg and Cheese Salad

Orange Sherbet Sponge Cake

Yellow Bonbons

Supper Menu

Ginger and Orange Sandwiches

Deviled Eggs Sweet Potato Puffs

Yellow Fruit Salad

Orange Bavarian Cream Lemon Drops

Yellow Bonbons

DEVILED EGGS

½ dozen hard-boiled eggs   1 tablespoonful butter
1 teaspoonful anchovy   Pinch cayenne
   paste   1 teaspoonful catsup
Salt

Remove the yolks from the eggs and work up into a paste with the butter, catsup and anchovy. Tomato or mushroom catsup may be used. When thoroughly blended and seasoned fill into the egg cavities. Serve on lettuce leaves or rounds of toast.

ORANGE BAVARIAN CREAM

2 cupfuls orange-pulp
and juice
1 cupful water
½ box gelatin

1 teaspoonful orange
extract
1 cupful whipped cream
½ cupful sugar

Dissolve the gelatin in half the water. Place the other half with the sugar over the fire and when at the boiling point stir in the gelatin. When cool add the orange-juice and pulp and extract. When it begins to thicken up stir in the whipped cream. Beat up until stiff, pour into a mold, turn out when ready to serve and garnish with orange carpels.